"This is a book that should be required reading for all high school and college students! It's jam-packed with information for not only the professional salesperson, but anyone who wants to get others supporting their efforts, dreams, and goals."

—Jessie Schwartzburg, author and speaker consultant

"In *Sell or Be Sold*, Grant will show you how to start with nothing and become wealthy with his proven strategies. This is a must-read for anyone who has the desire to be successful in sales and in life."

—Bryan Hardman, GSM, Monument Chevrolet

"This book is straight-to-the-point, clear talk that any professional will welcome and benefit from. Even if you are not a sales pro, it will sell you on sales as the most indispensable ability to make your own dreams fly."

—Harvey Schmiedeke, president, Survival Strategies

"*Sell or Be Sold* gives information that will cause you to think about where you fit into the 'spiritual' economy of the world and how you can grow to meet your life's needs and goals."

—Dale Christensen, CEO, NOI Investments

"The knowledge in this book will raise your income. Grant Cardone has created a masterpiece. It's pure oxygen for today's business world."

—John Mappin, founder, Metropolis Media Group

"No matter where you fall in the 'food chain of life,' you need to be able to sell yourself to others. Grant Cardone not only generates an awareness of this need, but helps you develop the skills to persuade others to see it your way."

—J. C. Walter III, president, Walter Oil & Gas Corporation

"I picked up *Sell or Be Sold* today and I have not been able to put it down. This book is nothing short of incredible—basics defined as never before and the truth of life and selling as one entity."

—John Hamlin, CEO, Hamlin & Associates

"I love this book, as it is a candid look at the truth! Following the path the author lays out will help anyone improve their life! I am having those close to me read this book!"

—Patrick J. Clouden, CEO, Consumer Energy Solutions, Inc.

"This last month I've been in survival mode, and after reading Grant Cardone's book, I am recommitting to my quest to master my game. Per his book, 'Knowing means Prediction, Prediction means Confidence, and Confidence means MORE SALES.' Thank you so much."

—Ron Palmer, DCH Group

"*Sell or Be Sold* is much more than I expected—the title really does not say enough about what the book is all about. It is truly about every aspect of your life. It is creative, motivational, and most important, it is very inspirational."

—Buddy Driver, director of training, Damson Automotive Group

"Reading Grant Cardone's book made me an emphatic believer that 'anyone can be a home-run hitter.'"

—Norm Novitsky, executive producer, BluNile Films

"*Sell or Be Sold* should be put in the hands of anyone who wants to run a successful company and should be the 'Bible' for anyone in sales. This book is so amazing I can't stop talking about it and telling people they HAVE TO READ IT."

—Kerri Kasem, radio personality

SELL
OR BE
SOLD

HOW TO GET YOUR WAY
IN BUSINESS AND IN LIFE

GRANT CARDONE

GREENLEAF
BOOK GROUP PRESS

Published by Greenleaf Book Group Press
Austin, Texas
www.gbgpress.com

Distributed by Greenleaf Book Group LLC

For ordering information or special discounts for bulk purchases, please contact Greenleaf Book Group LLC at PO Box 91869, Austin, TX 78709, 512.891.6100.

Design and composition by Greenleaf Book Group LLC
Cover design by Greenleaf Book Group LLC

Publisher's Cataloging-In-Publication Data
(Prepared by The Donohue Group, Inc.)
Cardone, Grant.
    Sell or be sold : how to get your way in business and in life / Grant Cardone. — 1st ed.
    p. ; cm.
    Includes bibliographical references.
    ISBN: 978-1-60832-256-5
    1. Selling. 2. Self-realization. 3. Conduct of life. 4. Success. I. Title.
HF5438.25 .C27 2012
658.85   2011941503

Part of the Tree Neutral® program, which offsets the number of trees consumed in the production and printing of this book by taking proactive steps, such as planting trees in direct proportion to the number of trees used: www.treeneutral.com

Printed in the United States of America on acid-free paper

16 17 18 19 20 21   14 13 12 11 10 9

First Edition

This book is dedicated to my father, Curtis Cardone Sr., who truly loved people and who was greatly respected by both his family and his community. My father had great admiration for salespeople and the sales industry, and he was a firm believer that selling was a prerequisite to a person creating success in any area of life.

CONTENTS

PREFACE

Since writing my first book, *Sell to Survive,* which was self-published, I have written three other books: *The Closer's Survival Guide, If You're Not First, You're Last* (*New York Times* bestseller), and *The 10X Rule: The Only Difference Between Success and Failure,* which I used to land a TV show.

As I wrote these books, I learned a great deal about what people could actually use, what was working, and, because of the input from people reading my books, I learned what they needed help with.

Sell to Survive has never been sold in a bookstore, yet it reached the top 1 percent of all self-published books by word of mouth alone. I have personally received comments and questions from thousands of people because of this book. As many of these readers have stated, this book turned their sales careers around completely. Others who did not consider themselves in sales suggested that this book allowed them to see where they had been missing it in their career with their goals to expand their businesses.

I believe *Sell to Survive* to be the most important book written on selling in the last fifty years and vital to every person who is interested in making their dreams a reality. We have taken that book and reworked it, added material, updated it, and retitled it: *Sell or Be Sold: How to Get Your Way in Business and in Life.*

Enjoy,
Grant Cardone

CHAPTER ONE
SELLING—A WAY OF LIFE

SELLING IS A PREREQUISITE FOR LIFE

Selling impacts every person on this planet. Your ability or inability to sell, persuade, negotiate, and convince others will affect every area of your life and will determine how well you survive.

No matter what your title or position is in life, or what your role is in a company or on a team, you will at some point have to convince others of something.

Selling is used every day by every person on this planet. No one is excluded. Selling is not just a job or a career; selling is essential to the survival and well-being of every living individual. Your ability to do well in life depends on your ability to sell others on the things in which you believe! You need to know how to negotiate and how to get agreement from others. The ability to get others to like you, work with you, and want to please you determines how well you will survive. Selling is not just a job—selling is a way of life!

Selling (Merriam-Webster's Collegiate Dictionary): The action of persuading or influencing another to a course of action or to the acceptance of something.

Who does this not affect?

When I say "selling," I'm talking about anything having to do with convincing, persuading, negotiating, or just getting your way. This could include debating, getting along with others, exchanging goods or services, convincing a girl to go out with you, buying or selling a home, convincing the bank to give you a loan, starting your own business, persuading others to support your ideas, or getting a customer to buy a product from you.

It is said that the number one reason a business or an individual fails is undercapitalization. Not so! The truth is, businesses fail first and foremost because their ideas weren't sold quickly enough and in quantities great enough, and therefore they ran out of money. *No* business owner can build a business without understanding this critical element called selling! Think of any action in life, and I assure you that there's someone at one end or the other trying to influence the outcome.

An example: A golfer has a six-foot putt. He putts the ball and then does everything he can to persuade that ball to go into the hole. He talks to it, he pleads with it, he makes motions with his hands, and he might even whisper a little prayer that the ball will drop. All the while, his opponent stands across from him and does the exact opposite. This example demonstrates that every one of us is always trying to influence a certain outcome.

The degree to which you can influence the outcome of events

in your life is the determining factor of your success. Those individuals who don't want to trust their fate to pleading, wishing, praying, and hoping must learn to persuade, convince, and negotiate successfully.

No matter who you are or what you do, you're selling something. It doesn't matter whether or not you call yourself a salesperson because you're either selling something or someone is selling you. Either way, one of the parties is going to influence the outcome, and it will either be you getting your way or the other guy getting his way.

A sale is made in *every* exchange of ideas or communication—there are no exceptions. Deny it if you will, but that won't change the facts. You're a salesperson, and you're one every single day of your life. From the moment you wake up to the moment you go to sleep, I assure you that you're trying to get your way. The fact that you don't have the title "salesperson" or that you aren't being paid a commission is only a technical issue. You're still a salesperson—and commissions come in many forms.

THE COMMISSION

Speaking of commissions: Every time you get your way, you've just been paid a commission. Not all payments are monetary. Some of the greatest achievements I've had in my life had nothing to do with money. Recognition for a job well done is a commission. A raise or a promotion at work is a commission. Gaining new friends is an incredible commission. Getting votes for a project you're pushing forward is a commission.

I find it comical when people tell me, "I could never be a

salesperson because I could never work on commission." I'm like, "What do you mean? Your entire life is a commission. There's no salary guaranteed in life. The whole world is on commission and the whole world is required to sell!"

It's been said that the best things in life are free, but I don't agree with that. The best things in life are those that come in the form of a commission for some extra, well-done effort! Happiness, security, safety, a great home, a great family, love, confidence, friends, your church, your community, and on and on—are all commissions for someone's hard work at selling others on a better way of life.

True love, the ultimate commission, is earned by those who find the right partner, take care of him or her, continue to create the relationship, and keep it growing. There's no guarantee that a relationship will get you love. First, you've got to persuade the person to take an interest in you. Then you have to find out what they want and what makes them happy. Then you have to produce it and keep producing it. But somewhere along the line, you have to sell the other person on the idea that you're the one that he or she can trust to create a life with. If you succeed and exceed the person's expectations, you will get the commission of love.

Health is not guaranteed in life. Health is a commission for taking care of yourself and your mind. When a person successfully sells himself on eating right, working out, and taking care of his attitude, he gets a commission of having good health.

The great benefit of children is also a commission of sorts and is not guaranteed to every marriage. You still have to convince your partner to have sex with you, and even marriage doesn't guarantee you sex. If you can't close your partner on wanting to have sex with you, then you won't get the great commission of children. Once you have the kids, you have to continue to sell. Concepts such as discipline, work ethic, education, good manners, and homework all have to be sold. If you don't do the selling, they will sell you. Kids are the best salespeople on the planet. They're passionate, relentless, and persistent closers, able to break down their parents' resistance until they get what they want!

The point is, selling is about life, and every area of life involves selling. The more consistently you can win at selling, the more commissions you'll get rewarded in life!

So get it! Everyone on this planet is involved in sales. There are no exceptions to this law. You're involved in selling almost every minute of every day. If this is somehow distasteful to you, then you have some misunderstandings about selling. When I say "selling," do you think of a fast-talking swindler who can sell anything to anyone? Maybe you immediately get a picture of some guy who's a confrontational, high-pressure type? Both of these images are negative extremes of selling and in no way describe the skills of a true salesperson. Confrontation and pressure are attributes of the amateur who doesn't understand sales and ends up resorting to unpleasant tactics.

When I discuss sales in this book, not only am I referring to the professional, paid salesperson, but I'm also covering the everyday use of basic persuasion skills and how to use them to get *your way* in life.

BEWARE OF FALSE DATA

The subject of selling, like any other subject, is full of false information that has been perpetuated over the years. This false data may be partly responsible for the poor impression of this profession and very needed life skill. "False data" is information that is not factual but is accepted as truth and passed along.

For instance, most of my life I wanted to own real estate and had a particular interest in buying apartment buildings. When I first got started, most of the people I talked to about apartments immediately told me that owning apartments was a nightmare and that I would have difficulties with tenants at midnight when the plumbing sprang a leak. Though tenants would obviously get upset if there was a plumbing leak, it is false data about owning apartments that actually causes people to lose interest in buying apartments. I've owned more than 2,500 apartments and, trust me, the renter is not the problem with owning them. Not having renters is a problem; leaky faucets are just an issue to deal with. Of course there are problems with owning apartment buildings, but so what? I assure you that the problems are minuscule compared to the rewards. People who knew very little about buying apartments used this false data as an excuse for me to not buy these buildings.

The whole subject of money is full of false data, most of which are passed on by people who give advice on money, but don't have any themselves.

When I was starting my first business, almost everyone told me how difficult it was going to be, how much money it would take, how risky it was, and how few businesses make it. None of these people had ever actually started a business themselves, but they had plenty of advice for me. You see, this is data that disregards all the successful stories of people like me who started their own business. I later started another company that required me to take on a partner. Multiple people suggested to me that most partnerships don't work out. Well, I can only tell you that while partnerships may be difficult, this business would have been impossible for me to operate without a partner. By the way, that particular partnership, which we closed on with a handshake, has lasted for almost fifteen years.

People tend to form opinions, give advice, and pass on myths when they don't actually have any personal experience. Much of the data they pass along hasn't been fully inspected for truth even though it's been passed on as truth.

Take urban legends, for example. A guy will swear to you that it was a friend of a friend's sister who disappeared on prom night twenty years ago and that her ghost now hitchhikes along the lonely road between town and the old cemetery. You'll hear that same story in multiple cities across the country. If you ask the guy to give you specific names and dates, he won't be able to provide them, yet just moments ago he was passing on this falsehood as though it were truth.

Many years ago, I was told not to move to California because "it was so expensive and the people were very strange." People who had never lived in California told me this!

The same phenomenon occurs with sales, and it's given the whole profession and the skill itself a bad name. It's a shame because everyone needs the skill of selling to get along in life, and the profession itself offers so much freedom and so many financial benefits. People continue to pass on the false information that selling is hard, that it's difficult to depend on commissions, that selling is sleazy, that you'll have to work long hours, that it isn't a dependable profession, that you can't rely on the income, and that it's not considered a "real" job! It's a shame, because selling as a profession offers a great deal of freedom and numerous financial benefits.

Most of the perceptions people have regarding sales are very rarely based in reality. Certainly any negative images you might have had about salespeople are based on the past—which would suggest that they're not particularly relevant to the present because they're in the past. If I'm talking about selling, persuading, and negotiating, you might get an image of a past experience or something you were told about salespeople that would take you out of the present conversation. You would be relying on some past decision, advice, or opinion for your information. All images based on the past have very little value in the present and definitely no value in creating a future.

SELLING—CRITICAL TO SURVIVAL

Regardless of your preconceived opinions, ideas, or evaluations regarding sales and salespeople, you need to fully adopt the idea that you're going to have to sell no matter what your position or job is in life. Whether you're rich or poor, male or female, on salary or on commission, you're always selling something to someone in order to advance. There is no exception to this rule and no way to escape it. But that doesn't mean that you have to start wearing polyester slacks and white patent-leather shoes and talk fast and pressure people to do what you want them to do.

Take a moment to consider all the different roles you play in life. Let's say you came up with wife, partner, employee, mom, teacher, church member, neighbor, friend, writer, and PTA president. I want you to look at each of these roles and observe how selling is involved in it. Maybe selling isn't your full-time career and maybe you don't get paid a monetary commission to sell products, but I assure you that you'll see how selling will affect your success in each role more than any other single ability that you possess.

The receptionist who wants a raise, the actress who wants the part, the guy who wants the girl—all rely on selling themselves, whether they know it or not. A professional salesperson who depends on sales for his livelihood definitely needs to know how to do this thing called selling. When you're driving to work and want to get off the freeway, you have to negotiate and sell the other drivers so you can access the off-ramp. When you find yourself buying a house and trying to convince the seller to sell at a lower price, you're selling. When you go to the bank to get a loan, you'll be selling the loan officers on why they should give you a loan. When the actor goes to an audition and hopes to get the part, no matter how well prepared he is, he'd better be able to convince the director that not only can he act, but he is the right guy for the part! Start preparing now because there's no way to avoid the fact that you'll need this skill to do well in life.

The skill of sales is so critical to a person's survival that I don't understand why it is not required study at school. The fact that it isn't taught in school, that it isn't required, or even offered, only further indicates the immense value of those who do learn this skill. It's my observation that the most important skills needed in

life aren't taught in school. I spent seventeen years getting a formal education, and I can tell you that I have learned more from
seminars, audio programs, books, and talking with other successful businesspeople at conferences than I learned in all my formal
education. No successful businessperson would exclude basic selling, persuasion, and negotiation skills from a list of those things
that helped him or her along the way.

A person's ability to persuade another is the only thing that
will ultimately ensure a position in the marketplace. Academic
records, grades, and résumés won't guarantee you a promotion
or advancement in life, but the ability to sell will. All students
should be required to learn basic persuasion skills, basic negotiating, and basic closing techniques, as these are fundamental to life.
No other set of skills will better determine the likelihood of a person getting a job, much less being a success in life, than the ability
to persuade, negotiate successfully, and convince others to act.

As an employer, I don't always hire the smartest person or
the most qualified person to fill a position. I'm much more likely
to hire the person who convinces me he can do the job. I look at
the person's ability to persuade before I look at the résumé. Will I
like being around this person? Is this person a winner? Does this
person exude confidence and a positive attitude? Can this person
convince others to take action? I'll hire the persuasive, positive,
and confident applicant hands down over the one who offers me
little more than a fancy résumé.

It's been said that almost a quarter of the population on the
planet is involved in selling, but whoever came up with this esti-
mation confined their thinking to an industry and a job type. It's
incorrect to think of sales in this way. Selling is an absolute must

for getting along in life. Breathing, eating, and exercising are not careers for most of us—they are fundamental requirements for living. So it is with selling. Most books written about sales are about the career of selling and exclude how vital it is to life.

My wife constantly asks me, "How do you always get your way with people?" The answer is simple—because I want to. I want to have a great life for us! Because I try to get my way? Oh, yeah! And because I know how to sell, how to persuade, and how to close the deal and get what I want! Whether she knows it or not, my wife is one of the best salespeople I've ever met. She's passionate, persistent, and always seems to get her way—and not just with me.

This book is going to teach you how to get your way in life!

CHAPTER ONE QUESTIONS

In the past week, what are three things that you accomplished that required you to use your sales skills?

1.

2.

3.

What does the author suggest is the number one reason a business fails?

What are three commissions other than money that you receive in life?

1.

2.

3.

What two skills will ensure a person's position in the marketplace?

1.

2.

CHAPTER TWO

SALESPEOPLE MAKE THE WORLD GO ROUND

SALESPEOPLE DRIVE ENTIRE ECONOMIES

Career salespeople are vital to the dynamics of any economy. Without salespeople, every industry on the planet would stop cold tomorrow. Salespeople are to the economy what writers are to Hollywood. It's been said that even God and the Devil need good salespeople.

Selling is the last great truly free-enterprise opportunity available today; in sales, an individual can work for himself, be accountable to himself, and make his dreams come true. Literally, with a pen to sign contracts and a commitment to excel, you can become whatever you want! For those who are willing to commit to selling as a career and to continue to learn how to master it, there are no limits. Do so and you'll be rewarded with all the treasures that exist. Learn the great art of selling and you will never be without work, because you'll always be needed by others. Learn how to control the entire cycle of selling from start to finish, and you'll have the confidence to go where you want, do what you want, sell whatever product you want, and know with complete conviction that you can have whatever you can dream.

The world would stop turning without salespeople. If a product isn't sold and moved on to the public, factories stop, production stops, there's no need for distribution, no need for storage, demand for shipping is reduced, and advertising stops. The burden of the entire economy of our culture today rests on the ability of salespeople. The economic engine of society relies completely on the ability to get products into the hands of consumers. If the consumers don't buy it, the factories won't make it.

Salespeople drive products, individual businesses, complete industries, and whole economies. Like many people, I went into sales when I got out of college because I didn't know what I really wanted to do with my life. I decided to try selling until I found a "real" job. I chose sales because it was easy to get into and I didn't have to make any life-changing decisions. Even after making my decision, my family, friends, and teachers rebuked me, saying that I should get a "real" job.

The problem for me was that the so-called "real" jobs didn't appear to pay "real" money—plus they seemed to be boring traps that sapped the life out of people. The only thing I could associate these "real" jobs with was the teachers who promoted them. Even today, these "real" jobs come with "real" titles, like doctor, lawyer, accountant, nurse, chemist, engineer, stockbroker, chiropractor, etc. But the funny thing is, all of these professionals have to sell themselves to others to make it in their careers. Their success in life is utterly dependent on one skill more than any other, and that skill is selling.

SALES OR COLLEGE?

It's a phenomenal mistake that the culture today doesn't value selling enough to teach courses on it. Not once throughout my entire formal education was selling introduced as an option. I wondered how respectable and desirable the field could be if it wasn't taught in school. If the subject isn't taught in the great "learning institutions" of the world, it must not be a real career. Right? Wrong! No one taught me about money or investing or real estate in school. But that doesn't mean that those subjects aren't valuable. Schools don't teach people how to make a marriage successful or how to raise children, either, and what could be more valuable than that?

Many young people attending my seminars have told me that they were torn between going to college and continuing with their sales careers. My response has always been the same: While the schools teach people very needed basics to get along in life and in the working world, no school can make a great person. You will learn absolutely necessary requirements in school, and you might make some great connections, but schools are not capable of making a person successful. Only by application will you or anyone else become successful or great in a field.

Survey the top one hundred most financially successful people in the world today, and I bet you can't find one who attributes his success to his formal education. Many of them didn't even go the traditional route. That is not to suggest that schools are bad or are a waste of time by any means; but higher education is not "the thing" that causes people to do great things. Look around and you will find the school systems we have today producing a workforce of people who are able to remember what they read rather than apply what they learned. While you will learn many very necessary basics in school, you won't learn how to balance a checkbook, increase your net worth, save money, negotiate a great deal, communicate, resolve problems, or increase your value in the marketplace. You will only learn such skills by seeking other information outside schools. That is what most people know they need to do in order to really improve their abilities. A basic education, while very necessary, cannot be considered an "end all." While there are some great teachers in the school system, it's unfortunate that due to the ridiculously low salaries, many of them are only regurgitating curriculums and forcing students to study courses and subjects that will never be used in their day-to-day lives. Ask any business owner what his greatest problem is, and it will always be the same. He can't find people who can think independently, who can solve problems, and who can increase his business and help him expand his company.

Schools teach students English, math, grammar, chemistry, history, and geography, which are absolutely necessary, but they never take the time to teach things as important as selling, persuading, and really meeting an employer's needs. The schools, for whatever reason, are just not set up to teach the things that may make the biggest difference. I don't know why that is, but I can tell you that I know salespeople who are making more money than heart surgeons, with far less liability and much less stress.

ALL PROFESSIONS RELY ON SALES

I know for a fact that for a person to have a great life, he'll have to know and apply the skills of any great salesperson. You can hire a doctor, a lawyer, or an architect, but you can't get along in life without the ability to communicate, persuade, negotiate, and close a deal.

These skills will prove more useful and vital than anything you'll learn through a formal education. I'm not suggesting that these other areas of knowledge are not valuable and worthy, because they are. I'm only demonstrating that selling is a valuable, worthy, and respectable profession and a vital life skill for all. Rather than being an hourly worker bee, you can become a highly paid individual with no ceiling on your earning potential. While others may have decided that sales isn't a respectable career, I can tell you that I've been able to spend time with leaders in many professions, from engineers and bankers to actors and film directors. Every one of those people has had to build a career around selling to get to the top of their industries. Of those top producers, every one has told me that they have studied books on negotiating, selling, and persuading. Why? Because they understand that those skills are vital to their success.

Every person, no matter what his profession is, relies on selling. The politician wants to appeal to you and your interests so that you'll vote for him in the polling booth. The public speaker is hoping to convince the audience that his approach is the right one. The employee desiring a promotion will have to sell the boss on his value to the company. The coach has to sell his team on the idea of winning the game. The real estate agent must convince you to buy a house or to give him the listing. The mortgage broker wants you to refinance for the third time. The banker wants you to invest money in the bank's mutual funds. The waiter is selling the special of the day. The clothing salesperson wants you to buy the suit along with three shirts and two ties—and also wants you to apply for the department store's credit card.

Selling never ends, and it includes everyone. Those who can sell, persuade, and close are the ones who survive the best, regardless of the line of work.

I'll let you come to your own conclusions about why selling is neither respected as a profession nor taught in schools. Maybe it's because there have been a handful of criminal salespeople over the years who have ruined the reputation for all. These are not salespeople; they're crooks. But you'll find criminals and con men in every field, including medicine, law, dentistry, teaching, politics, and certainly psychiatry.

I'll tell you the fact of which I'm sure: No person will ever gain true power and stature in the world without the ability to persuade others. The ability to communicate and convince others is an asset for you; the inability to communicate is a liability. No matter what your ambitions are, you are required to communicate with others, and the better you can communicate, the more people will agree with you. The more you can get others to agree with you, the more you can have your way in life. The more you get your way in life, the more you will enjoy life.

CHAPTER TWO QUESTIONS

What are three freedoms that come from selling?

1.
2.
3.

What are four things that depend upon salespeople?

1.
2.
3.
4.

In your own words, describe the importance of sales to the economy.

What does the author suggest is either an asset or a liability when it comes to selling, and how does this affect your life?

PROFESSIONAL OR AMATEUR?

THE PROFESSIONAL

Step into my world and let me unveil the secrets of the professional seller and how you can become one. Even if selling isn't your career, you should be a professional seller in order to get more out of life. I tell attendees in my money seminar, "If you want to get rich, learn how to sell." I became a professional at selling when I was twenty-six years old, after years of research and intense study on the subject. The hard work was well worth it, and the rest of my life changed as a result of my learning this little-understood life skill. Every business I have started, every dollar I have earned, and all the great things that have happened in my life are a result of learning this ability.

Three-quarters of the world's population have no clue that the successes they will experience in their life and career depend solely on selling. If they don't know how to sell, they will not be successful. While selling may not be your main occupation, hopefully by now you are convinced that selling is essential to your life. No dream can ever become a reality without successfully selling it to others.

Professional: A person who is engaged in a specified activity as his or her main paid occupation rather than as a pastime.

It's been my experience that 99 percent of all "professional" salespeople have only a slight idea of what selling is, much less how to actually determine and predict results. What I've said is not meant to offend you in any way, but to inform you. If it does somehow offend you, then keep reading. Sometimes the truth is tough to hear, and this book will put you in control of your profession, put you in control of your customer, help you increase your income, and transform you into a true professional. Most real pros do not even call themselves salespeople; rather, they call themselves litigators, negotiators, moderators, business owners, inventors, politicians, coaches, fund-raisers, agents, actors, entrepreneurs, financial planners, and so on. Consider Benjamin Franklin, John F. Kennedy, Martin Luther King Jr., Bill Gates, Martha Stewart—they are just a handful of the real pros of selling.

THE AMATEUR

Amateur: A person who engages in a pursuit, study, science, or sport as a pastime rather than as a profession, or one lacking in experience and competence in an art or science.

I've met hundreds of thousands of salespeople over the past

twenty-five years, most of whom were amateurs and did not know the first thing about selling. Is selling just a pastime to you, no different than watching television? Do you lack experience and competence in this field? Are you not clear about what you're doing while negotiating? Do you struggle to get your way in life? Do you think there's no way you could ever be a salesperson? Do you have disdain for this thing called selling? Do you hate rejection and even the idea of selling another? If any of these questions describe how you feel about selling, then we have some work to do.

I can show you how to become a professional, but first you have to get clear on two things: (1) Selling is critical to your survival regardless of your career, and (2) you must decide to become a professional and give up any idea that it's something for others and not for you. You have to decide that you want to start getting your way in life. Quit thinking that it's up to fate or the gods. It's up to you. You will have to shift your thinking to understand that your very life and every dream you have ever had depend solely on your ability to sell. If you aren't getting your way, then quit making excuses. Decide now to learn everything there is to know about the only secret to success—sales.

THE GREAT SHORTAGE

For thousands of years, salespeople have been amassing wealth and accumulating riches, and these same opportunities still exist today. It isn't real to most salespeople that they can amass fortunes, but that's due to the short-sighted view of the opportunities available for the great and dedicated salespeople.

While there may or may not be shortages of water and oil on this planet, I assure you there are vast shortages of highly committed, highly dedicated, and great salespeople. This is good news for those who choose to become a great salesperson, for the world awaits you with its fortune. While there are hundreds of millions of people who call themselves salespeople, there are only a handful who are really "the greats." The difference between mediocrity and greatness lies in being committed to the profession and being consumed by the desire to be great and the dedication to learn the trade. Despite the popular belief that there are limits in sales, I assure you that the only limits you'll face are those that exist in your imagination.

The truth is, you can get paid whatever you want to. There is no ceiling. You can decide what products you'll sell, who you'll sell them to, and who you want to work with. The truly great salespeople who stand out above the rest aren't even really in the same profession as the masses. They think differently, act differently, and work differently. To them the job is effortless because they understand how to reach their goals. They're paid immense fees compared to their peers. They make selling look easy, and others are certain that their success is the result of some "gift" they were born with. Nothing could be further from the truth. I've never met anyone that reached stellar levels of success who got there because of luck or some sort of God-given talent. They're successful because they have mastered the trade.

When the economy crashes, "the greats" may experience small dips in production, but they always survive, whereas the amateurs lose their jobs. Great salespeople don't have ceilings on their earnings and they know that their income depends solely on their ability to get in front of customers, make themselves known, get agreements, close sales, and reproduce those results over and over again.

Only a handful of people ever take the time to really learn this game and master it. When I was twenty-five, I made the commitment to know everything there was to know about the game of selling. I was finished with pumping myself up every morning with enthusiasm and *hoping* for great results. Enthusiasm is great, but it's not a replacement for *knowing*.

The amateur goes out and plays golf every Saturday with his boys, but he can't play with a master who truly *knows* the game of golf.

The person who knows what he's doing and understands every nuance of his career doesn't have to *get* enthusiastic; he *is* enthusiastic. When you really, truly know something, you can predict outcomes. He who can predict outcomes has true confidence and freedom.

CHAPTER THREE QUESTIONS

What is the difference between a professional and an amateur (in your own words)? After you answer, check to see what you left out by referring to the book.

Write down three qualities you have been told there is a shortage of in salespeople.

1.

2.

3.

Now write down three qualities that you have observed there is an *actual* shortage of in salespeople.
1.
2.
3.

What are the three differences between mediocrity and greatness, as stated by the author? (Check off the elements you need to strengthen.)
1.
2.
3.

When the economy dips, what is the significant difference between what happens to "the greats" and what happens to amateurs?

CHAPTER FOUR
THE GREATS

COMMITMENT

So how do you become one of the greats in your field, one of the masters? The very first step, and the most important one, is to commit all the way!

Commit: To devote oneself completely to something.

This inescapable truth is that to be truly great at anything, you must devote yourself completely. If you are a career salesperson, you have to devote yourself, your energy, and your resources to a career in selling. If you aren't a career salesperson, you'd better get it to your core that your success still depends on this skill, and then you'd better learn it. You have to convince yourself that this is the thing you have to learn in order to get your way in life and that this is where you are going to make your riches.

How does a person commit?

What I do is eliminate any and all other options and devote

myself to learning everything I can about the topic. I become a fanatic, 100 percent absorbed, all in, a Super Freak! I stop questioning and get in all the way. Furthermore, I discontinue looking at other options.

Committing is as simple as picking a place to park your car. Find a spot, pull in, and get out of the car. You don't keep looking for another space in which to park. COMMIT AND BE DONE WITH IT. Committing is when you make a firm decision, you quit wondering, and then you follow through on your commitment with actions.

Once you've fully committed to a partner in life, it's good advice to quit looking for new partners. You take what you have and make everything you can out of it. Can you find someone prettier, smarter, and happier? Probably, but that's not committing. Committing means you are in all the way, you are done looking, and you make the person you have committed to the prettiest, the smartest, and the happiest. I would rather commit to the wrong thing all the way than commit to the right thing only halfway.

Commit and be done with it!

GREENER PASTURES

The guy who thinks the grass is greener "over there" is the same guy who never commits to taking care of the pasture he already has. He winds up mediocre and miserable. What was he even doing looking at another pasture in the first place? He already has one that needs to be mowed. Remember, while there may be greener pastures, they're green because someone committed.

Weeds grow in every field, and if you don't commit to it all the way, you'll neglect it. When you neglect it, you'll start to dislike it, and then you'll start peering over the neighbor's fence and thinking that what he has is better. It's only better because he committed. So commit to your career, commit to learning about selling, commit to your product, service, and employees. Commit to learning everything you can and watch how much green your career will produce for you.

Whenever I commit myself to any line of action, I get immediate results. When I'm not committed all the way, I find that results are delayed or nonexistent. If I'm committed 100 percent to the customer before me, I get results. But when I'm with one customer and thinking about another customer or wishing I had a better customer, I'm unable to make the best of what I have. Commit and commit all the way.

When I give seminars I often wear a small gold pin on the lapel of my jacket that says "100%." A salesperson asked me if I wore it for my customers to see. I explained that while customers do see it and are intrigued by it, I don't wear it for them. I wear it for myself. I wear it to remind myself to commit all the way. I don't get dressed for my customers; I get dressed for myself so that I feel good, so that I'm dressed professionally. I wear that pin to remind myself that I'm 100 percent committed.

Commitment is a personal thing, and it's the indisputable requirement for getting results in life and separating yourself from the herds. At the age of twenty-five, I had been in and out of sales for five years or so and I realized that I was still looking for another career. No commitment equals no results. I had not made a commitment to sales yet, and I was not proud of my position or the work I was doing. How could I be? I was only average at best. I was average because I was not committed. Because I was not committed, I was not getting results. Because I was not getting results, I did not like my job—it was all a vicious cycle.

To the degree that you aren't proud of the job you're doing, you won't be successful; and the degree to which you are successful will determine how proud you are of your career. The career you are in is not the problem—your commitment is the problem!

I decided one day (after years of being mediocre) that sales was not the problem—I was. At that moment I devoted myself to learning everything there was to know about sales. My goal was to stand head and shoulders above others in my field and to no longer be compared with them. I decided to become a professional and be different than the "typical" average, mediocre salesperson. That was the moment when everything changed for me, and it changed immediately and magically. Right away my energy changed, my dress changed, my actions and habits started changing, my language changed, and my results changed. Immediately, my pastures became green and my potential exploded. It was almost spiritual! No, it *was* spiritual. It was so dramatic—and that is the magic of commitment.

If you want to be successful at anything you have to commit. You've got to be in it 100 percent with no other fish to fry. A "burn the ship" kind of mentality is what it takes to get you to a place where you'll do things that will ensure results. Get into the game as though your life depended on it, because your life does depend on it. The life that you've been dreaming of depends on you getting in all the way now. This is how I approach anything when I really want results. This is how I approached the career of selling, and the moment I did that, my life changed.

I'll never forget the first time I experienced the magic and power of commitment. One summer I was working on an off-shore crew boat that serviced oil rigs. We were off the coast of Louisiana, and we used to sit around waiting for the rigs to call on us. When we weren't actually working, we'd spend our time fishing off the side of the boat. On one particularly lucky day, we reeled in hundreds of red snappers. As we packed them in what little ice we had on board, I listened to the other crew members, who were planning to take their share of the fish home to eat.

For some crazy reason, I offered to buy up everyone's fish with the idea that I'd go out and sell them. At the time I'd never sold anything and I didn't know anything about fish sales. I didn't even know to whom I was going to sell them. All I knew was that my gut instinct was telling me that someone would want to buy those beautiful fresh red snappers.

With hundreds of snappers piled in the back of my truck, I realized that I needed to create a market, find some customers, and figure out how to convince them to buy my fish. I had to think fast because the ice on the fish was melting, and I was going to lose my paycheck and my inventory if I didn't move the product right away. As I thought about where I might find customers, I remembered how the Bible salesmen used to come knocking on the door of our home and how committed those guys were. It was getting late, and I decided that if the door-to-door approach was good enough for the Bible salesmen, it was good enough for me. As the ice continued to melt, I blasted through neighborhood after neighborhood announcing that I had fresh fish. Knocking on doors, I rapidly explained that these fish had been caught in the Gulf that very morning and they were the best that money could buy. After I'd covered the houses in the area, I went to businesses, where I found more prospects and sold the rest of the fish. And I did it all before the last of the ice was gone. I learned about the value of commitment that day. I had a fanatical, have-to-get-it-done-and-no-other-options level of commitment!

Commitment = Results = Happiness

I made more money selling fish in a few hours than I had made doing hard labor for *two whole weeks*, and it all came after I had made the commitment to sell those fish. I had put myself in a position where I did not have any choice. I had to sell them or lose them. It was a do-or-die situation. After that experience I was "hooked" on sales, but I did not become a professional for seven more years.

The first thing you have to do is to commit yourself to selling as something that is vital to your life regardless of your career (but especially if you are in sales). Commit right now and watch what happens. Commitment is like magic, and nothing great will happen until the commitment is there! Most people do not attack their projects with "I-have-to-get-it-done-now" urgency and therefore they do not get it done. Most people never commit like fanatics, and therefore they never become *fantastic*.

THE POWER OF PREDICTION

The moment I transitioned from an amateur to a professional (following my decision to commit and become dedicated to my career), I began studying the whole area of selling. I started taking notes on every exchange I had with my customers. I even recorded these experiences on audio and video. I would later study the material like a football team reviews playbacks of games. I didn't know it then, but that was how I gained the ability to predict.

To predict is to know what's going to happen next. I stumbled across this skill and found myself gaining the ability to accurately predict the outcomes of situations *before they happened.* I started to know exactly what I had to do every day to create a certain amount of income. I was gaining the ability to predict exactly how many people I had to get in front of in order to sell a certain amount. I then discovered I was increasingly sure of what to say and how the prospect would react to what I said. I was able to predict objections and handle them *before they even surfaced.* It was as if things had gone into slow motion and I knew what every player on the field was doing and would do in the moments to come. The ability to predict is the first thing that happens when you become a professional, and when I reached this level of ability, I knew I was on my way to great success.

Prediction is the great unknown—and very often unrecognized—asset of the professional. I've never heard it spoken about, but I know it exists. If you've ever read about any of the great athletes, they talk about this same phenomenon whereby they are able to *know* what's going to take place before it even happens. Wayne Gretzky and Michael Jordan have both noted the experience of being able to predict where the play would move to and how it would turn out.

Years ago, I was selling a product to multimillionaires and quickly discovered that I had only a very short time in which to make my presentation to them, as time was of great concern to these people. In fact, time was more valuable to them than money. With one prospect, I knew exactly what his objection would be when I got him on the phone: "I'll give you sixty seconds, son." Having predicted correctly, I handled him without having to think about what to say or do. Because I had studied prospects like him and had formulated and prepared solutions, I was able to be responsible for the exchange and get results. This prospect, who started out difficult, became one of the best clients I have ever had and later launched my career in sales training.

How does one gain the skill of prediction? You have to start looking at everything that's happening, observe it accurately without emotion or blame, and make a note of it. The ability to predict comes from assuming responsibility for what's going on around you and believing you can control it. You have to pay complete attention to and record encounters; then you'll start to see a finite set of patterns.

When I started recording my phone calls and making notes of every exchange I had with customers, I immediately tapped into my ability to perceive patterns, and then I started being able to predict. It was so easy and so fast. I carried around an "objections" notebook and wrote down every customer objection. Later I would study my notes and start to see that most of my customers were making similar comments. My awareness was raised and I was able to come up with solutions. It was amazing how fast I became aware of what was going on. One customer would tell me something and I'd write it down. The next customer would say the same thing and I'd write that down, too. When I began observing and taking responsibility for what was happening to me, I was able to predict what the prospect would say. More important, I was prepared to handle him. I had control because I knew. To know is critical to success, as knowledge equals power in life. To *know* means you end up with fewer noes. Fewer noes means a better life!

My production almost doubled from the simple action of observing. My confidence soared as my knowledge increased, and so did my income. Prediction! I could see the future, not because I was a psychic, but because I'd observed the past accurately. I didn't realize it at the time, but I realize now that the ability to predict is one of the first benefits received from committing all the way. I had become responsible, aware, alert, and solution-oriented, and was able to predict! Until you become a dedicated student, you cannot gain the skill of prediction. All masters (in any career) are able to predict accurately.

Once you get some sense of possible situations that can occur, start taking notes and record everything you can. Record yourself on video so you can watch yourself. I started looking at what I said, my facial expressions, my responses, my tone, my voice, my gestures, and wow, there was so much to learn. I became addicted to knowing all that I could! To predict is to know, and to know is to handle situations correctly. This will increase confidence and increase sales. To sell successfully is to enjoy your job, which means you will continue to expand with more sales. Winning begets winning.

THE ONLY REASON YOU WON'T LIKE SELLING (AS A CAREER OR IN LIFE)

Do you want to know the only true reason someone doesn't or wouldn't enjoy selling? There is only one real reason—and it is not what you've been told. It's not because someone doesn't like rejection. After all, who does? It's not because they're lazy. Everyone is lazy when they fail, and most people are trying to avoid failure. It's not because they don't like people. We all like people when we're successful with them.

The only reason a person doesn't like what he's doing is because he doesn't know what he's doing! He isn't winning, and that's because there's something that he doesn't know. The doctor who can't save lives won't like being a doctor. The teacher who can't get her students to learn will sooner or later become disenchanted with teaching. A salesman who can't close deals won't like selling. Therein lies the only reason you would not like being a salesperson. When you don't understand something, you aren't in control, and when you aren't in control, you aren't going to like what you are doing!

I met a guy named Scott Morgan back in 1995, and we were considering a new business partnership. I was giving a presentation in Vancouver and suggested that he come up for the weekend to talk about our new arrangement and get in a little skiing. Scott had never skied before, so I suggested that he take a beginner class. He arrogantly puffed out his chest and decided that a beginner class was beneath him. The next morning the two of us were at the top of Mount Whistler, one of the steepest mountains in North America. Scott looked down and then at me, and we both knew he was in big trouble. He knew nothing about skiing, let alone how he was supposed to get down the mountain. While I admired his courage, I observed that he didn't understand the value of training. Scott spent the entire day making his way down that mountain, and to my knowledge, he never put on a pair of skis again.

When he finally made it to the bottom, I suggested that we start a training company so that salespeople would never have to experience in their careers what he had had to experience on that mountain. Scott and I have been business partners for many years now. He's one of the most persistent people I know and has made a full-time commitment to help others through training so they can successfully take their careers to the mountaintops.

TO QUALIFY AS GREAT!

All greats are able to predict the outcome of any given situation, and great salespeople are able to determine and predict their own income. If you are unable to effectively and consistently increase your income as a salesperson, you are not a professional, and there is something that you don't know and aren't able to predict. It seems like it would be fairly important to be able to predict the objections and stalls that your prospects will give you; if you can't, it means you are not truly a professional, and it will show up in lost sales.

Regardless of how long you have been doing this, if you're losing more than you're winning, then you need to realize that you're an amateur and it's time to kick up your commitment a notch and become someone who *knows* what he's doing! You say, "Man, you're being harsh on me! I'm just going through a cold spell right now." Wrong! You're making excuses; the reality is that your cold spell is due to your own lack of understanding of your profession. You've been sliding by on amateur skills, and those skills are showing up in your results. Anyone can sell when everyone is buying the product, but when there's competition and the economy tightens, the amateurs start crying and the professionals continue to prosper. The major difference is that the professional is committed and knows what he's doing, while the amateur is not committed and does not know.

A boxer is considered a professional boxer if he's paid. But if he loses every match, people won't continue to pay to see him fight, and he'll return to amateur status. He'll be knocked down to his true rank. Most businesspeople are being knocked down by the economy due to their ranking—their lack of commitment and not knowing how to sell.

In my opinion, you don't have to be able to predict what you have to do to raise your income. You are a professional when you can predict results and get them. If you know your game, you don't have to rely on luck—instead, you can achieve consistent success and can compete with others at the top. Pay just happens to be the reward given to those who reach the top.

There are many professional mothers who aren't paid for raising their children. On the other side of the coin, just because a woman is a mother doesn't mean she's a professional mother. There are mothers out there that you wouldn't hire to babysit your own kids.

Just because you cook doesn't mean you're a Cordon Bleu chef, but you can be a professional even though you're not paid for it. My sister is a professional cook, not because she earns a living doing it, but because she *knows* what she is doing, she *knows* the kitchen, *knows* her appliances, *knows* her timing, and *knows* her recipes. It's not just the preparation of the meal and the fact that the food tastes good. Hell, I can duplicate her recipes, but the amount of mess I create compared to the amount she creates, the time I take, and the effort I use isn't even close. I'm an amateur cook, and she's a professional. She has the ability to predict all that goes into preparing a meal and I don't. This ability comes from committing to being aware and observing the scene completely.

Just as there are lots of cooks and mothers, there are also lots of so-called salespeople. But just because someone is engaged in the business of selling doesn't make that person a professional.

If you're a professional golfer it means that you've qualified by playing in tournaments against others and have qualified based on your abilities to produce results. And just because you're a professional doesn't make you a great.

To become one of the greats, you have to practice, not just play. To become a great golfer, for example, you have to commit every fiber of your being to the game and still know there's more to learn. Do you see the difference?

Most salespeople are amateurs, some of them are professionals, and only a few are greats. Ultimately, it comes down to the level of commitment and dedication you have. The greats can predict, a skill that comes from committing, observing, and preparing solutions. To the degree that you can predict, you can respond appropriately. Prediction is the great trait of the great salespeople.

The more you're able to predict with accuracy, the more you'll be prepared to handle situations. It's like driving: If you know what the other drivers are going to do, you can avoid accidents. It's not just about driving your own car. You've got to be able to predict what other drivers will do. Using the tool of observation will help you learn how to do this.

Can you remember a time when you knew nothing about your job, but you still got it done? It wasn't consistent, your income went up and down, but you still made it happen. You made a sale but didn't really know why. You missed a sale and you were mystified for days. Can you remember a time when you used sheer persuasion, even begging or pleading, and the buyer felt sorry for you and you made the sale? Leave that for the amateur and the underpaid professionals and start observing now so you can predict!

Observation is the only way you'll acquire a strategic understanding of the sales process, and it's the only way to develop your prediction abilities and become one of the greats.

Remember, no matter what your job or role is in life, you need the ability to predict. You're either getting your way in life or you're not. Even if you're not a salesperson per se, start observing where you are not getting your way and start taking notes.

Those who understand selling will get their way in life and those who don't, won't! Are you ready to become a great? Are you prepared to pay the price and do the work? If you are, I assure you that it will change your life dramatically, quickly, and forever!

CHAPTER FOUR QUESTIONS

Define "commitment" (per the definition the author used and look up each word).

Write down an example of something you didn't fully commit to and the result.

Write down an example of something you committed to completely and the result.

What is the skill of prediction? How is it gained?

What is the only reason a person would not enjoy selling?

THE MOST IMPORTANT SALE

SELLING YOURSELF

Only to the degree you are sold can you sell. This is a critical and unavoidable fact that cannot be missed if you're to become great at what you do. This fact also happens to be one of the most important tools you'll ever have as a salesperson, and it can be used to monitor your career. The bottom line is, if you're not selling to some degree, *you're not sold.* If sales are slow, you're not sold. If you're not getting your way, you're not sold. If you've got some other excuse, you're not completely sold.

In order to become a great salesperson, you have to sell yourself on what you're selling. Make this the most important sale of your life and continue making that sale over and over to yourself. You have to sell yourself completely!

I know salespeople who know the game but are not completely and absolutely sold on their product, service, or company. Because of their lack of conviction, they are not consistent producers. You've got to be absolutely convinced that your product, your company, your services, or your ideas are superior to all others. Many salespeople believe that their products are superior, and while many products tend to offer similar benefits to yours, you have to be sold that your product, service, or idea is somehow superior. You have to be 100 percent certain that what you're selling is better than all other options. The fraud can't get consistent results because he is not completely sold on his product.

This one point is critical for greatness, and you cannot negotiate it in any way. You have to be utterly convinced and believe in what you're selling so strongly that you become unreasonable. That's right: Unreasonable, even fanatical! You've got to be so convinced that you won't even consider any logic suggesting otherwise. I am not saying that you should be arrogant about the product's superiority, but that you should be completely sold on it. You must never allow the consideration to enter your mind that anyone else could even compete with you. That's not to say that others won't try, but you have to be so convinced and so sold on it yourself that you won't consider or allow others to consider any other option.

Throughout most of my selling career I've sold more expensive products than my direct competitors. I have also gotten more money for similar products than my competitors have because I believed so strongly in my service, my level of care, and the superiority of my products. Whether this was true to others or not was less important to me than my own conviction. While I've sold products that were priced higher than those my competitors were selling, I've never asked a buyer to pay a price that I wasn't fully sold on myself, and that, I believe, is the only way to achieve higher prices.

I have been accused of asking astronomical prices for some of the products I've sold. The critics thought that I was asking a high amount in the hope that I'd get more than the product was worth—the idea of "if you don't ask for it you won't get it." But the truth is, I've never asked a high price just for the sake of starting high. I decide on a price because I'm so convinced of the product's worth that I would pay that price myself to have it!

CONVICTION IS THE MAKE-OR-BREAK POINT

One time I put a house up for sale and the best realtor in town told me it was worth maybe $6 million. I told her to put it on the market at $8.9 million because the location was irreplaceable, and I believed it was worth that much. I was 100 percent convinced that the house was worth that price because I could have actually made sense of paying that price myself. I sold the house two months later for almost the asking price, and everyone in the neighborhood loved me. The new owner went on to sell the same piece of property a year later for $10 million. It wasn't until after I became convinced of the value that others agreed with me.

The conviction that you have regarding your product is more important than the conviction that others have about their facts and figures.

The word "conviction" is defined as a "firmly held belief." It comes from the word "convince," which is derived from the Latin word "convict," meaning "to conquer."

Conviction is the ability to be so firmly sold on your beliefs that you demonstrate to your buyer with such complete and utter certainty that no other choices appear to be available.

A sale is made when your conviction and belief about something are stronger than another's, at which point they give up some of their conviction. That's the moment when the sale becomes possible. I'm not even talking about a product or service at this point. I'm talking about the conviction of the individual himself. The real issue becomes who is more sold on what he believes to be true. Who is the most believable and the most convincing? It will always be the one who is most sold!

A highly trained U.S. Army Ranger is so deeply sold on his mission and so sold on the cause that he's able to do things that would appear superhuman to others. He's convinced of the need to perform at this level and he does. Why? Because he's sold on his mission. He doesn't think; he operates. He doesn't have to think because he's already decided. He believes in it to his very core, and because of this he's able to achieve the impossible.

Alexander Graham Bell was considered a lunatic when he talked about inventing a device that would transmit the human voice over long distances through wires. He was told that his invention, called the telephone, was impossible. But that's the interesting thing about the impossible. It's only impossible until someone makes it possible! Look at photography, flight, space travel, e-mail, the Internet, and on and on. All of these things were considered impossible once upon a time—until someone became sold on them being possible.

Why is it that some people do things that others wouldn't dream of doing? It's because they are sold on the idea that it needs to be done for some reason. To the degree that they are sold and become unreasonable in their quest, they will succeed.

While it's unfortunately promoted in our society to be reasonable and sensible, these characteristics will not serve you in sales or in life. If you really want something great to happen, you've got to be unreasonable, even if it means convincing yourself beyond reason that what you have is better. We aren't talking about some trivial pastime here like riding bicycles! Anyone can learn to ride a bicycle. We're talking about becoming a great in your field, and to do that you have to be completely and unreasonably sold on yourself, your product, your company, and your ideas.

You might be wondering, "To get to this point of being unreasonable, do I have to be crazy or insane to be successful?" The answer is no. You need to make a decision to be unreasonable. If a person acts insane, it doesn't mean he's insane. It means that he decided to act insane.

If you're unreasonable in your belief and sold to the degree that you see no other options available to the customer that would make sense, it doesn't mean that something is wrong with you. It means that you're unreasonable in your convictions.

Being unreasonable means that you are sold on what you're selling, and it is your conviction alone that will sell others on it.

You must be completely IN if you are to fully maximize the opportunities before you. Do not even attempt selling to someone else until you yourself are completely sold. To the degree that you aren't sold, you'll have difficulty selling to others. Anytime you find yourself having trouble getting your way, look no further than your own degree of conviction in what you're selling.

Perhaps you allowed your certainty to waver, or maybe something entered your head that made you doubt yourself or your product just a tiny bit. Whatever it was, find it and throw it out like yesterday's garbage.

If you wouldn't buy the product or if you have any negative considerations about how it benefits others, to that degree you are guaranteed to fail. You must be sold. You must get rid of all negative considerations and believe that it's the right thing, the right product, and that it will benefit the person you're selling it to. It's critical that you do everything possible to convince yourself that your product must be purchased and that it must be purchased from you at your pricing.

Why should someone go into debt to buy your product? Why should they choose your product instead of someone else's? Why should someone do it right now and not wait another second? Why should they buy your product for more money rather than a similar product for less? Why should someone buy it from you rather than the guy down the street? Why should they choose your company over another? If you can't instantly answer these questions, you'll struggle along because you're not convinced. If you were completely sold, you would have immediate responses to each one.

Become so thoroughly sold on your product that your conviction is irresistible to others. This is not meant to suggest that you lie to yourself, if that was even possible. I've personally met thousands of high-producing salespeople over the years, and never have I met a top producer who got to the top by deceiving others. What I'm suggesting is that you take the time to sell yourself before you try to sell someone else on how your product is superior to others.

OVERCOMING THE NINETY-DAY PHENOMENON

I've met many salespeople who tell me that they started selling a product and did well with it for ninety days, but then suddenly found themselves unable to close a deal. What happened? Management will tell you that the person has gotten lazy or that he's gotten too smart for his own good. Okay, so he got lazy. But why? He wasn't exhibiting laziness for the first thirty days, and he couldn't have gotten too smart for his own good because ninety days at any job won't make you smart by any means.

What I believe happens to cause this ninety-day phenomenon is that either the individual was being told to do something that wasn't aligned with his own personal standards of ethics or he's now trying to sell something that he's no longer completely sold on. Maybe he doesn't believe in the product anymore. Maybe he has disagreements with management, or something that he's promising. He's refraining from doing something that he was doing for the first ninety days. Something changed!

Maybe he got some information about how the product doesn't help people or how it doesn't do what he's been promising. Maybe he didn't close a deal and started wondering why, and then made up the wrong reason for it and continues to use that incorrect reasoning. This happens a great deal. Salespeople come up with wrong answers and then continue to use these wrong answers when trying to solve future problems.

Whatever it was that happened, the ninety-day wonder is basically no longer sold. Actually, he is sold—he's just sold on something else. In fact, what he's now sold on is that it's a bad idea to sell this product, and so he starts not selling the product! Not selling is also a form of selling, just in reverse. Something has affected him to the point where he's motivated not to sell rather than motivated to sell. Do you get it? Something went out in his thinking and he's no longer convinced.

When a salesperson's production drops, this is the first thing you should look for and rehabilitate. This individual must be revitalized and resold on the product, the company, and the services. Go over all of the ways that the product is superior and how it will benefit others. Find out if there's some counter-intention, disagreement, or false information about the product, service, or company that's in conflict with the salesperson's beliefs. Once you've handled that, ask him how he felt about the product or service when he was doing well selling it and you'll soon find him motivated and closing deals again.

It's incredible how many salespeople tell me stories about the competitor that undersells them and practically gives products away or how the very product they sell can be bought on the Internet for less. I recently read a book called *Secrets of Successful Selling* that talked about how competition had reached levels never before seen and how customer awareness had reached a point that required salespeople to operate at levels never before considered. The book was written in 1952, which just goes to show that there's always been competition and there always will be. The problem isn't product knowledge, competition, or smarter customers; the real issue is whether or not you are fully sold on your product.

Become so sold, so convinced, so committed to your company, product, and service that you believe it would be a terrible thing for the buyer to do business anywhere else with any other product.

Are you so sold on your product that you think it's detrimental and unethical not to convince someone to buy from you? Get to that point and watch your production freak out! When a customer doesn't buy your product, do you actually feel bad for him and lose sleep feeling like you've screwed him over because he didn't buy it from you? If you were really sold, you would feel like that. That is sold! The person who is sold completely won't let people not buy, because that would be a violation of his own integrity! Reach that level of being sold, and I assure you that people will buy from you.

You might ask yourself, "But what if I'm not convinced that I have the best product or the best service?" Then get convinced, and do it right now! Do whatever it takes to believe that you're offering the greatest product and the greatest service. Find the plus points and sell yourself on them completely.

Let us take as an example an unhappily married man who wishes he had a better relationship. Perhaps he hasn't been paying attention to his wife and he's lost some of his commitment and passion over the years. What happened? He basically isn't sold anymore. At one time he was completely sold on his wife, so sold that he suggested they spend the rest of their lives together. Somewhere along the line he stopped selling himself on the marriage.

If you want your marriage to work better, then convince yourself that you have the best spouse on the planet. How is your spouse the best? What sets him or her apart? What makes that person unique, different from any other human being on this planet? What are you sold on? She burns dinner, she looks terrible in the morning, and she's got big ugly feet! Setting the negatives aside, look at what sold you on her in the first place. Sell yourself on her all over again. Find the plus points and ignore the imperfections. Get back to being sold and doing the things that you were doing early on and watch the change. You'll be amazed to see what happens. Suddenly she isn't burning meals anymore, she looks great in the morning, and she's gone out and gotten a pedicure and a nice pair of shoes.

GET SOLD OR BE SOLD

Should you lie to yourself? Of course not; but you've got to get yourself sold no matter what! Rather than lying to yourself, a better alternative is to do what a champion does: Champions decide to win the game with what they have to work with. They don't change teams. They make the most of the assets and strengths available to them. They play the cards they've got and they make the most of the pot. They don't lie to themselves; they convince themselves that the only solution is winning, and they commit to one outcome only—success!

Focus on winning whatever game you're playing in life. Sell yourself on what you need to do today to make today great, to make your relationships great, to make your neighborhood great, to make your life great, and to make the sale. Find every plus point and sell it.

David beat Goliath not because he had any real chance of being able to, but because he sold himself on the idea that he had to. Did he lie to himself? Absolutely not. He became convinced that his survival depended on taking down the giant. This is what you must do. Get sold and get committed to the fact that you're offering a superior product or a great service that can't be beat. You've got to make it so true to yourself that you can say it to others with such conviction that no one would even think of challenging you.

PUT YOUR MONEY WHERE YOUR MOUTH IS

One time a real estate agent was trying to convince me that a particular investment was a great deal and a great opportunity for me. He kept going on and on about what a fabulous investment this property was. But I wasn't convinced because he didn't *say* it convincingly. He lacked the believability of someone who is completely and thoroughly sold on his product. Like any customer who isn't sold, I started questioning him. It wasn't the deal that I was unsure about as much as it was the salesman who was pitching it. Something just didn't add up with the way he dressed, how he presented his pitch and the rushed, loud sales talk. He sounded like a "salesman," not like someone who was completely and securely confident about his product.

Finally I asked, "Since you continue to tell me how great an investment this is, how many have you bought yourself?"

With a dumbfounded look on his face, the salesman quietly answered, "None."

You might be thinking that my question was unfair because maybe he couldn't afford the product. Look, if it's a sure thing, why not pool all the money you, your kids, your parents, and your friends have and buy it? If it's a *sure thing*, you're not putting anyone at risk. If your product is a great deal, wouldn't it make sense that you'd be willing to buy it yourself?

By owning the product you're selling, you're demonstrating your certainty to others by your actions, and actions do speak louder than words. That's the difference between a "salesperson" and someone who's completely sold. It's unbelievable to me how many people sell products that they don't own themselves! Every product I've ever sold, I first bought myself and was proud to tell people that I owned it.

Obviously, you can't buy every single product that you sell, but you've got to be *willing* to buy it.

You have to be so sold that you use your product, consume your product, and would sell the product to your loved ones. Otherwise you're just a mercenary selling whatever for the highest fee.

ICE TO AN ESKIMO?

I consider myself to be a great salesperson, but that doesn't mean I could sell any product. To the degree that you're in disagreement with some product or idea, you won't be able to sell it.

For example, I couldn't sell ice to an Eskimo, as the saying goes. Why? Because it would be unethical for me to sell ice to an Eskimo since I just don't see the need. I couldn't and wouldn't sell psychiatric drugs of any kind, no matter how much money you paid me. I could never convince myself that drugging people could possibly solve their problems or make their lives better. I can sell only that which I'm completely sold on.

A finance and insurance salesman at a car dealership was having difficulty selling his products, and he came to me for advice on improving his sales. I began by asking him when he had last bought a new car. He said that he'd recently purchased one, and he went on to tell me how much he loved it. Because he was sold on that car enough to buy it himself, his conviction for the product shined through when he talked about it. He was speaking from the heart. I went on to ask him which of the finance and insurance products he'd purchased with his new car (credit life, accident, health insurance, and warranty). With a chuckle, he admitted that he hadn't bought any of those products because he didn't want to spend the extra money on them. The truth was, he didn't buy them because he wasn't sold on the very products he was selling. Because he wasn't sold, he wasn't able to get others to buy the products from him. You might think, "No, he was just saving money!" Look, if you are completely sold, you won't concern yourself with the money. You'll buy the product! There is no exception to this rule ever!

If you're having a similar problem, it's an easy one to resolve and doesn't even require that you learn anything about selling. All you have to do is buy the products you sell and then watch your sales go up. People are inclined to do what others have already done. People will follow you to your chiropractor, consult your doctor, hire your maid, or go to the movie you recommended— all because of what you did, not what you said. To the degree that you're sold, you will take action, and to the degree that you take action, you will be successful in selling others!

I assure you that the finance guy I mentioned earlier would be more successful if he were able to demonstrate through *action* that he'd already made the same investments himself. He would have been able to look at his customers with full conviction and show them that he'd done what he was asking them to do; that he'd put his money where his mouth was because he was sold himself. By the way, he took my advice and his income quadrupled.

THE VITAL POINT

The vital point of having salespeople who are sold is missed by 90 percent of all management. Go to an Apple store and ask the salespeople how much they like their products. Those people are so totally sold that you'd think it's a religious movement. The Apple people aren't using PCs at home; they're sold on Apple and you feel it when they present their products.

I went to a very high-end steak restaurant and I asked the waitress which steak was her personal favorite. She told me that she was a vegetarian! Hello? Is anyone home in management? What is this person doing in a steakhouse?

I would never hire a salesperson if he wasn't willing to buy and use the product himself. I also wouldn't hire a salesperson who wouldn't buy the product because he doesn't have the money. If he truly doesn't have the resources, let's get him a credit card or a payment plan and sell him the product so he can tell others how he loved it so much that he went into debt to buy it!

Additionally, I wouldn't hire a salesperson who wouldn't spend money. If a person won't spend money or tends to be really cheap in how he spends his money, he'll always have trouble getting other people to spend their money. I assure you that the less hung-up you are on money, the easier money will come to you. I know of salespeople who are so tight that they still have their first commission. While they brag about this frugality, I am convinced they would have reached much higher income levels had they not been so tight regarding their own money, because more people would have given them more money.

If you won't buy it yourself, then you're not sold yourself! If you can't pass the simple test of being willing to buy your own product, you'll never be able to sell others in large numbers.

You have power when you're sitting at the closing table and can look the prospect dead in the eye and show him that you've already made the exact same purchase that you're asking him to make. Your personal conviction and believability will take your career to new heights when you're fully sold. Buy the product yourself and you'll become a miracle closer and will be able to handle objections that ordinary salespeople can't! Be totally sold on the products, services, and the company you work for and watch your prospects turn into customers!

CHAPTER FIVE QUESTIONS

What is the most important sale you have to make?

What are four things you have to be sold on in your life?

1.

2.

3.

4.

Define "unreasonable."

What does the author suggest is the make-or-break point in selling? (Define it.)

Write down three lessons you were given in life that suggest you should be reasonable.

1.

2.

3.

How convinced does the author suggest you become about what it is you are selling?

CHAPTER SIX
THE PRICE MYTH

IT'S ALMOST *NEVER* PRICE

If you were to survey all of the salespeople in the world, you'd find that most of them believe that the number one reason they lose a sale is price. This is absolutely not the case, and, in fact, nothing could be further from the truth.

Price is not the buyer's biggest concern. It's actually at the bottom of the list of reasons why people don't buy. Most sales are lost over unspoken objections—not the obvious and apparent objections like price, payments, or budgets, but the ones that the buyer doesn't voice. Getting the sale isn't about money; it's ultimately about the buyer having confidence that the product is the right one.

If there is a price difference, the customer wants assurance that your product has advantages in excess of the cost difference.

THE PRICE EXPERIMENT

Most salespeople believe that if the price were lower they could sell more. But the truth is, they wouldn't sell more because they haven't correctly named the problem, and therefore they can't get the correct solution. I once had a salesperson who said that if the price of my seminar tickets were lower he'd be able to sell twice as many. Even though I knew that what he was saying was bordering on idiotic, I practiced the first rule of selling—"Always agree with the customer"—and told him that I often wondered the same thing and, in fact, would be willing to test his theory.

So we offered a Grant Cardone seminar in Detroit with tickets at one-tenth of the normal price. Detroit has always been one of our best-attended seminar markets, and the person who made the suggestion about the price cut was thinking that we would have the biggest audience ever. There was only one stipulation to our deal to properly test out his little idea: He could sell the tickets only by sending out a marketing piece offering the seminar, the date, the price, the website address, and a phone number to call. He was not allowed to do a full sales presentation. The reality is, if you take the price that low you won't be able to afford to do a presentation anyway.

That seminar had the lowest attendance of any I have given in twenty years. It didn't even cover the cost of my airfare, and the salesperson's commissions didn't cover the cost of the mailers. I asked the audience why they thought so few people had come, and they said that they hadn't thought I would actually be there in person; they had expected that the seminar would be a video feed of me. If the price gets too cheap, people won't see any value in the product. Additionally, if price alone were the reason people buy, then the company wouldn't really need salespeople and that would be a problem for 25 percent of the population.

Success will always take a professional salesperson who takes the time to sell features and benefits.

IT'S LOVE, NOT PRICE

After the experiment with the cheap tickets, I doubled the original ticket price, and attendance at my future seminars increased by more than 100 percent!

Price is almost never the issue for buyers, even when they say it is. More often than not, the real issue is love and confidence. Do I love this product? Because if I do, then I'll pay whatever it takes. Is the buyer 100 percent confident that this product will get him what he wants? Will this service do the job? If the buyer is head over heels in love with the product and can't live without it, he'll buy it regardless of price, assuming he can find the money to pay for it. If the buyer has full confidence that the product will solve his problems and get him a real solution, he'll buy it at almost any price. People will give their right arm for love, and they'll give their last dollar for a real solution.

If you've ever lost someone then you know what I'm talking about. In that moment when you found out you'd lost someone special, you'd sell everything you had and go into debt for multiple lifetimes, just to have that person back in your life. Why? Love, baby—love!

You have to get your buyer to want your product more than

he wants his money! He's got to want the product or the solution more than he wants the numbers in his bank account. Discovering what he's trying to accomplish and demonstrating how your product solves his problem is the essence of how you close the deal. Certainly there's the issue of the product being out of someone's price range, but that's the point I'm trying to drive home. If they really love it and it will really solve their problems, they'll figure out a way to come up with the money.

You can't put a price tag on someone or something that you really love. And if you've ever had a serious problem in life, money was no longer your concern. Getting rid of the problem was. Give 'em love, solve a problem, and you will get the money.

If the customer can afford the product or service but isn't buying and is harping on the money, it always means that he has other concerns that must be handled. If he were completely sold, price would not be the issue.

While your prospect may be verbally objecting to price, other thoughts are most likely going through his mind: *Is this the right product? Is there a better product than this? Is this the right proposal? Will this truly solve our problems? Will my people use it? What will others think of me buying this? Is this something I am going to really use and enjoy? Will this company really take care of me and service us? Am I better off buying something else? Will something better come out next week? Do I know enough? Do we have all the information? Should we get an "X" instead? Should I join the country club? Am I better off with the money in the bank than investing it? Is this going to be a mistake like past decisions?*

If these considerations are handled to the buyer's satisfaction, price will no longer be the issue. The product or service that you're selling will obviously create different concerns for the decision maker, but trust me, regardless of what it is you have, it almost never comes down to just price. To the degree that you understand this, you will be successful.

Let's say a guy is buying a birthday present for the love of his life. He finds something he thinks his girl will love, but tells the salesperson that it costs more than he would like to spend. What he's actually saying is that he isn't completely sold on the product being the perfect gift for her. He either doesn't love it himself or he's not sure that it's something she will love. This product is not yet making him feel good enough or certain enough to pull the trigger and buy the gift. In this case, I would acknowledge him, tell him I understand that it is more than he wants to spend, but ask him for the opportunity to actually show him something a bit more expensive just for fun. He said it was too much—he didn't say he didn't like it and he didn't say he couldn't do it! Also consider that when he said it was too much, he could mean that it was too much for that product, rather than that he couldn't do it. Maybe, just maybe, he'd rather spend extra money and get a gift he loves more.

MOVE UP, DON'T MOVE DOWN

Most salespeople make the mistake of offering something for a lower price when faced with price objections. This is an incorrect solution based on the false belief that price is the reason people don't buy things.

When you move the customer down in price or offer him something cheaper, he's less likely to want that next product if he didn't want the first one. This will cause the buyer to think that you have no solution and that he's just wasting his time. By moving him up rather than down in inventory, you'll get him thinking in terms of value, and you'll find out whether his objection is valid or not.

If he believes that his girl will love the gift and he really wants to make her happy, then showing him something more expensive will actually get you closer to a sale. Remember, he wants to make good decisions. At this point he'll either demonstrate that the first product was the wrong choice by the simple fact that he's now looking at the more expensive option, or he'll tell you that he needs to move in the other direction with something that costs less. Either way, you've now got him shopping with you, not negotiating with you. You could even show him a completely different line or product with the knowledge that you could always move back to the original. You want to exhaust your inventory, not your price!

I remember a customer who once told me that my product cost too much money and I was unable to close him. He left me and bought a product for $150,000 more from my competitor. When he said it was too much money, he was really saying it was too much for the solution I was offering. You will discover that as many price objections will be solved with more expensive solutions as are solved with lower prices.

When I can't close a sale, I'll always try to move the buyer up to a bigger or more expensive product as the first solution to price objection. Although this might not make immediate sense to you, I assure you that it will prove successful. If the customer will at least consider it, I know I'm on a product that he still has questions about. This is called "closing with inventory." I've had thousands of customers tell me that it's either too much money or that it's over the budget, or they get that uncomfortable money look on their face during the close. I'll immediately move that buyer up to a more expensive product. Why? Because they're telling me that it's too much money for that product or service or that they're not sure it will resolve their problem. The buyer would rather pay more and make the right decision than pay less and make a mistake.

Every consumer has made mistakes before, and this is the number one reason why they hesitate to make decisions. It is the fear of repeating a mistake; it is not the fear of spending the money. It's the angst about making the wrong choice or buying the wrong product or making a decision that doesn't create the solution they were looking for more than it is price.

Always show your buyers how they can spend more as a solution to price—this will determine whether or not you're dealing with a real price objection. The worst outcome is that the more expensive product will make the one they're looking at seem more accessible, which will actually build value and substantiate the price. Never buy into the talk of the mediocre salespeople around you who believe that price is the most important issue or who promote the idea that if the price were lower they could sell more! Just look at their results and then disregard their advice.

One time a charity asked me if I would help out with some fund-raising. The members told me about this one prospect who had the wherewithal to make a sizable donation and was supportive of the charity, but they were having trouble getting him to make a financial contribution. They'd been working on him for a year and hadn't gotten a penny. I asked them how much they'd been trying to get him to donate and discovered that they'd been asking for $10,000. I suggested that they might have been asking him for too little. Maybe this prospect didn't like making small contributions and that it might be easier to get a larger one.

One woman looked at me with disbelief and said that this man was one of the cheapest people she'd ever tried to get a contribution from. So I took the prospect aside and in ten minutes had him closed to contribute ten times what they'd been trying to get for a year. He wasn't cheap by any means except in the mind of the fund-raiser. In fact, he was one of the most generous people I'd ever met. He told me that he hadn't contributed anything to the charity in the past because he didn't feel that $10,000 would really make a difference. All I did was ask him for the right amount, the amount that *he believed* would make a difference! The higher contribution actually solved his problem.

Tip: Your prospect is never the problem—*never!* Salespeople, not the prospect, are the ultimate barriers to every sale.

SALESPEOPLE, NOT CUSTOMERS, STOP SALES

You have to get this into your head: *Price is not your problem*—you *are your problem!* Customers do not stop sales. It is salespeople who stop sales from happening. You, not the customer, are the barrier to the closed deal.

Give the prospect a product that he loves or a service that solves his problem and you'll get the close once he has full confidence in the product or service and you.

There will be times when you'll have to handle the buyer on

money. Sometimes I remind a person, "While I agree it's a lot of money for a gift, there's no shortage of money on this planet. But there is a shortage of people who've found the love of their life and who know how to show their appreciation for that person. Be grateful you've got someone to love. Now, how would you like to handle this?" Now that's selling! If the buyer is totally convinced it's right, he will chew off his own foot to have it!

If the buyer who's saying it's too much money found out that he had a disease and was going to die, but this product would save his life, what would he do? He'd find the money, buy the product, and save his life. Why? Because he's completely sold on the need! If the need is important enough and he has confidence in the cure, if the love is great enough, price will not be an issue.

When buying a house, for instance, the unspoken objections that the realtor won't hear will be, "Is this the right house? Is this the place that's going to fulfill our needs? Will we be happy here? Is this going to be a good investment? Do I really love this place? Can we do better? If we're going to spend this much money, why don't we spend a little more and get our dream house?" The last one—let's spend more money—describes about 50 percent of all buyers who are concerned with price. The same buyers who use price as an objection will often go out and spend even more money, not less! Remember, many times when a buyer says, "It's too much money," what he's really saying is, "It's too much for this product"!

Remember the story about a house I sold for 50 percent more than the realtor said it could possibly bring? When the buyer came to the house, I knew she loved it the moment she walked in. Later she insisted on having an appraisal done because her manager said she was paying too much. I explained to the buyer that while I understood she wanted an appraisal, it would be a waste of money because the house wouldn't be appraised for the price she was paying. I told her that the house was overpriced and because of that it wouldn't appraise. I went on to tell her that I'd paid too much for the house when I bought it, that the people before me paid too much when they bought it, and that the next people after her were going to pay too much for it. Because of the location, it had always sold for more than it appraised for and everyone would always overpay for it. The buyer decided not to have an appraisal done and bought the house. She lived there about a year and a half and sold it to the next people for too much money. It's never about price; it's about love or confidence that the product will solve problems.

$4 COFFEE AND $2 WATER

To be an effective salesperson, you have to believe in human beings. You have to have a positive outlook about people. You have to believe that people are good and that they want to make the right decision. Your buyers are just like you—they spend money they don't have, they go over budget, they work hard for their money, they've made good decisions and they've made bad decisions. Like you, they want to avoid bad decisions and make good ones. People want to feel good about themselves and their decisions.

If you're selling a service to a business owner, he wants to know that he did the right thing for his business and that what he paid for is going to make a difference for his company. If you're selling a product, consumers want to have certainty that they'll be happy with it and that when they use it they're going to feel good, look good, and be admired by others because of the choice they made.

If people don't buy from you, I assure you it's almost never about the money or the budget, but about something you didn't uncover. If it were all about price, please explain to me why people stand in line for a $4 cup of coffee when they could make an entire pot at home for almost nothing. Explain why people spend $2 on a bottle of water when they could simply get water from the tap for free. Explain why someone spends thousands of dollars on season tickets to the ball game when they could watch it on television. Explain why someone would go out and buy a sports car when they could take the subway to work and arrive there in half the time. Explain why you bring your kid to a professional when he cuts himself rather than stitching him up yourself! Love, baby—love!

Consider how many times you've paid more than you could afford and you *loved* it! Consider how many times in your life you went over budget because you found something that you weren't even looking for and decided to buy it on impulse.

Remember, it's almost never about price.

CHAPTER SIX QUESTIONS

What does the author suggest is the main reason people don't buy something?

Give two examples of when you told someone that you couldn't do something and used price as the reason when there was another objection that you never voiced.

  1.

  2.

What are the two main reasons people will buy something?

  1.

  2.

Write down three things people buy everyday that they love but don't need.

  1.

  2.

  3.

Write down three examples of times when you bought something you could not afford because it solved a problem or you loved it so much you had to buy it.

  1.

  2.

  3.

What does the author suggest is the best way to justify a price when there is an objection?

CHAPTER SEVEN

YOUR BUYER'S MONEY

THERE IS NO SHORTAGE OF MONEY

Before you ask customers for their money, there's something that you need to get straight about the subject. Millions of people on this planet have the false idea that there's some sort of money shortage. But the truth of the matter is, there's more than enough money to go around. In fact, there's a surplus of it.

Did you know that there's enough money circulating on this planet for every human being to have a net worth of $1 billion? One billion dollars! Are you getting your share? If you're not, it's because you're thinking in terms of hard work and limits, not in terms of abundance.

Look out at the Pacific Ocean and observe the infinite energy created there. The Pacific never stops. Go out there and get as many buckets of water as you want. How many buckets can you take? If you took as many bucketfuls as you wanted, would there still be plenty of ocean? Absolutely.

Look at how much money is in the marketplace. How many people own homes, own cars, pay telephone bills every month, and buy clothes and food? There are endless amounts of money, and if we ever get close to running out, they'll just print more—thus inflation!

Get over the idea that there's a scarcity of money because there isn't! There's plenty of money to go around. If you start looking for prosperity and abundance, you'll see that these things exist all around you.

ALERT! If others have a difficult time getting money from you, you'll never find it easy to get money from others. Many of the best and highest-paid salespeople I've known are the most generous people I've ever met. They're less scared about money, not because they have it, but because they understand that money is to be used, not possessed. Because they know this, they don't have trouble getting others to part with it.

YOUR BUYER AND HIS MONEY

Your buyer becomes quite funny when it comes to decision time and giving you the money. It's as if money somehow identifies him or he feels he'll be different once he gives it to someone else. When it comes to actually parting with the money, buyers can act strange and start making excuses; they might generate odd stories and even alter the truth a bit. The trained professional knows how to stay in the deal, knows how to handle objections and stalls, and knows how to persist and can do so without appearing to pressure the customer.

It's even funnier when you consider that most people aren't giving you money; they're merely transferring numbers from one bank account to another. In most cases they aren't even paying for it; someone else is. But they say, "I can't afford this." Of course they can't afford it—that's why we have banks!

I've had people tell me that my price is too high when it wasn't even their money on the table. When the actual money guy got involved, he immediately said "yes" and never once mentioned the price.

Some of the most difficult buyers I've ever been involved with later thanked me profusely for hanging in there with them, working through the price issues, and helping them make the right decision. Love your product, love your service, love your customer, and love yourself enough to learn how to "hard sell." If you need some help handling your buyers' price objections, then get my complete audio program on closing the deal. It will change your life.

SECOND MONEY IS EASIER THAN FIRST MONEY

I discovered the second-money phenomenon by accident one week when I was on fire, selling everybody that I called on. It was one of those freak moments when everything was easy and effortless. Every prospect I was working with was buying from me, and it seemed as though I'd walked through some magical closing portal in the universe. I'd spent hours selling this executive team who were trying to make sense of the product being affordable for their company. They finally submitted to my logic and persuasion and agreed to make the purchase.

Upon acceptance of that product, I decided to see if I could move the executives up another level, as I truly believed that it would be a better investment for the company. I knew that they'd already gone over budget, but I had to try anyway. I suggested to them that since they were already paying more than they were comfortable with, why not go all the way and move up another level? They looked at each other and turned to me in astonishment. "Actually," one of the guys said, "we were going to ask you to do just that. We're already paying more than we can afford— we'll just have to produce a little more to make it work." In that moment I'd stumbled across one of the great secrets of selling: *Second money is easier to get than first money.*

Startled by this discovery, I reflected on times when I'd been out shopping for a product and took forever to decide on that one particular item. But once I finally made a decision and bought it, I found myself buying another eight items on the way out of the store. This phenomenon is common among consumers. Once the flow begins, the buyer becomes more open to making more purchases. It is my belief that the consumer is actually using the second and follow-up purchases to support the rightness of his first decision.

Why does someone refer you to his or her dentist? To help the dentist? Maybe, but more likely they refer you because convincing others to go to the same dentist supports the rightness of their own decision. Everyone wants to know they're doing the right thing, and the other-purchase phenomenon supports their actions and gives them the reassurance that what they did earlier was correct. Find one woman walking down Rodeo Drive in Beverly Hills, carrying just one shopping bag. You probably can't. They'll all be laden with multiple bags. Case closed!

Another example of this is a customer who walks into a travel agency with the idea of taking a cruise. He spends four hours with the travel agent looking at all of the cruise line brochures while trying to figure out which package will best suit his needs. *Should I go take a cruise to Europe, Mexico, Alaska, or the Caribbean? Should I take a five-day cruise or a two-week cruise? What is the best cruise line and who has the best ships?* Once the customer decides on a destination and purchases the perfect cruise vacation, the climate is right for the travel agent to step in and offer additional products. There are accommodation upgrades from an inside deck cabin to an ocean-view suite, the island tour excursion package, travel insurance, airfare upgrades, and on and on. Because the customer has taken the plunge and bought the first item, he's going to want to be right about his first decision, making him available to purchase additional products and services in order to support that initial decision.

I was raising money for my church and working on a prospect who had been very resistant to make any contribution. When I finally got him to agree to make a donation, I congratulated him. As I watched him write the check, I looked at him and said, "You know you're going to do more than that before you die. Your heart's in the right place. You're a generous man. Why don't you just do the rest now." He looked at me and said, "You're right." He tore up the first check and wrote me another for twenty times the amount that he'd initially decided on!

If you've ever seen someone at a restaurant complain about the price of a steak, and then turn around and order a bottle of wine that's twice the cost of the meal, you know what I'm talking about. Or how about the person who whines about paying ten bucks for a movie ticket and then spends another twenty on popcorn, soda, and candy? Have you ever heard a guy complain about how high his car payment is? This is the same guy who later customized the car with 22-inch wheels, a custom paint job, and a stereo system that you can hear from three blocks away! Of course, he had to charge it to his credit card at 18 percent, and the payments on the wheels, paint, and audio amount to more than the payments on the car. Yay for the second money! Learn this one and your life will change forever!

THE MORE THEY SPEND, THE BETTER THEY FEEL

Your prospect, regardless of what he says, always wants more, not less. Believe it or not, people love to spend money, and the more money they spend, the more they enjoy spending it and the more they will enjoy their decision. Show me one person who has ever come in under his or her budget when buying a home, car, furniture, equipment, clothes, a vacation—anything. That person doesn't exist. Consumers want to take home lots of things, not just one thing. They want to brag to their friends and neighbors that they spent the most money and bought the most expensive thing. *People love showing off.* If they didn't, there'd be no market for sports cars and designer clothing. Anyone can buy a leather purse that will last just as long as a designer handbag, but people know that the designer brand cost ten times more because of the label and insignia. This is America, a nation of consumers and one-uppers. Good or bad, we like to buy and we like to be seen buying. Therefore, the second purchase reinforces that the first purchase was the right decision.

Second money is easier to get than the first money. People will tell you, "Don't get greedy; don't complicate the close, just finish it or you might blow the deal with your attempts to get the second money." Nonsense. That kind of thinking is for the little, mediocre salespeople of the world, not for you! Second money is for those who want to take their game and their income to the next level and want to do it in half the time.

You'll spend 90 percent of your time eating the main course and 10 percent eating the dessert. Get the first sale wrapped up and then focus on the second sale—it's the dessert.

This is a monster technique that works like magic. All a salesperson has to do to unlock the door of second money is get over his own fear of blowing the deal by *asking* for it!

Remember, money is a mental issue, not a shortage issue.

CHAPTER SEVEN QUESTIONS

If others have a difficult time getting money from you, what will happen to you?

Write down some of the strange things you have done when it came time to part with your money.

1.

2.

3.

What is the easiest money there is to get and why?

Why would someone feel better spending more rather than less?

Why would money be a mental issue, not a real shortage issue?

CHAPTER EIGHT

YOU ARE IN THE PEOPLE BUSINESS

THE PEOPLE BUSINESS, NOT THE "X" BUSINESS

Manufacturers are constantly pushing product awareness and product knowledge because they believe this is the weakness of their sales force. They think if the salespeople just understood how the product worked and the benefits of it, they'd sell more. While it's true that salespeople must have a great understanding of their products, one must not forget that it's *people* who buy those products. That's why it's vital that salespeople know about people first and products second. I've known salespeople who understood the ins and outs of the product and every detail, but were unable to close the deal because they had inferior understanding of people. Being superior in product knowledge but inferior regarding people knowledge equals minimal results.

If you understand the product before you understand people, you're putting the cart in front of the horse. Realize that you're in the people business first and the product business second. Certainly, you need product knowledge. You have to know the benefits of the product and how it compares to others, but first and foremost you need to understand people and what they want before you can sell the product or show someone the benefits of it.

Most salespeople I meet spend too much time selling the product and forget that selling is 80 percent people and 20 percent product. This is illustrated by people buying inferior products every minute of every day. Why is this? Because people buy for reasons other than just the product benefits.

A person stops in at a convenience store after work and buys a carton of milk. Is that brand of milk the very best they can possibly drink? Is it the best price in town? That person doesn't know and doesn't care because it's not the carton of milk that he's buying. It's the convenience he's buying that will get him home to his family as quickly as possible.

The shoeshine guy at the airport does not understand that it's not the price or the quality of the shoeshine that keeps people from stopping at his booth. He doesn't realize this because he thinks he's shining shoes. The reason the businessman doesn't stop for a shoeshine is because he doesn't need a shine; it's not because of the cost. The businessman is concerned about missing his connecting flight. If the shoeshine guy advertised SIXTY-SECOND SHINES, he would have to expand his booth to handle all the business. To hit the right button to close the sale, you have to realize that you are in the people business, not the shoeshine business.

Learn to think like customers think. Products do not think, feel, or react. People do.

I live in Los Angeles, and my wife and I buy gas from a station on Sunset Boulevard where the owner comes out, greets us by name, fills up the gas tank, cleans our windshields, and gives us a bottle of water for free! Am I buying the gas or the service? Is this about people or the grade and quality of the fuel that is being put into my car? Is the owner selling people or gas? Where do you think we fill up? If you understand people, then you'll get the right answer. The owner of the station understands that he is not in the gas business, he is in the people business—which is why we continue to buy from him.

It has been said that people do not care how much you know until they know how much you care. I believe this is true, and I can validate it with commission checks. I never consider that I am selling a product, but I do consider that I am helping a person make the right decision. I have sold fish, cars, clothes, real estate, videos, jewelry, investments, and even ideas. I found that I did best when I was interested in the individual—the "human being" who wants to enjoy life and solve a problem by buying my product.

More often than not, salespeople launch into their pitch without knowing anything about the customer, which is a surefire way to miss the sale. What is important to the buyers? What do they need? What is the ideal scene for them? What is it they are actually trying to accomplish with a purchase? What is it that really makes them feel good? If they could get everything they wanted, what would that be? These are the questions that will let you know how to sell them.

Take interest in the client instead of interest in selling him something. When a buyer goes out looking for a product, he doesn't care how much you know about the product, he only cares about himself: His time, his money, and doing the best thing for himself. He cares most about himself at this time; you and your product are way down on his list of concerns.

THE MOST INTERESTING PERSON IN THE WORLD

> "I may not be the most interesting person,
> but I am the one I'm most interested in."
> —Anonymous

People are far more concerned and interested in themselves and their family and in doing the right thing than they are in having another product, no matter how much they need or want it.

If you don't show as much interest in the buyer and his concerns as you do in selling, he'll know that you are only in it for the commission. Be more interested in the customer than you are in yourself, your sales process, your product, or your commission and you will make more sales.

My wife and I recently met with a veteran high-end real estate agent who was showing us a house. As we were walking through the property, I began to tell the agent what was important to us, at which point she cut me off and continued to pitch the house. You'd have thought this agent was a rookie to the business, but on the contrary, she'd been in real estate for more than twenty years. Maybe that was part of her problem. She had joined the ranks of those in the *real estate* business and had forgotten that she was in the *people* business.

Ninety percent of all salespeople don't take the time to listen to the prospect or find out what that person is actually looking for! While this agent has been very successful compared to others, imagine what she could sell if she were genuinely interested in people and in determining what they wanted and needed! It would certainly save her time, as she would then know what to show me and how to sell me. It's easy to do, but you have to be interested and you have to know how to communicate. Not talk, but communicate! True communication requires finding out what is important to people so you can identify what they actually want and then deliver it. What do people value? What is important? Why is it important? How do they want to be spoken to? What is going to cause them to take action?

Once I was selling a condominium to a couple in Tucson, and I observed that the husband wouldn't look at me. After a couple of minutes, I bluntly asked him, "Excuse me. Why won't you look at me?" He was shocked at first, but then he started talking to me. I took interest in him, and when I did he started communicating with me. I asked him what his ideal scene was with regard to a place to live. The question allowed him to open up, and he told me everything they were looking for. During the conversation, the subject of golf came up, so I showed him where the closest course was. He went on and on talking about golf, and he didn't stop until he'd signed the documents. I barely even sold the condo; I just took interest in him, got into communication with him, and made him more important than the product I was selling. I found out what was important to him, I listened, and then I closed.

COMMUNICATION = SALES

If you don't get into communication with the buyer, you have no chance of ever making the sale. The dictionary defines "communication" as *a process in which information is exchanged between individuals through common symbols or behavior.*

Just talking about your product is not communicating, since there's no exchange of ideas between you and the buyer. In sales we're interested in communication that gains access to information, which can be turned into action. To gain information means that your communication should include lots of questions. What do you want this product to do that your present one doesn't do for you? What would your present product have to do so that you would be satisfied with it? On a scale from one to ten, how would you rate what you are using/own now? What would make it a ten? This type of (interested in you) questioning will help you discover what the buyer wants, what he needs, and, most important, to what he assigns value. Additionally, asking questions demonstrates your interest in the individual, and people want to know you are interested in them, not just in a sale.

Years ago I was shopping for a computer and the salesperson started reeling off details about the speed, the memory and storage capacity, the megabytes, and all this technical information that meant nothing to me. I walked away from him feeling like a zombie from all of the technological terms and misunderstandings that he spewed at me, and I didn't make a purchase. A week later I wandered into another store and met a real salesperson who approached me and immediately started asking me questions rather than spewing data. He asked me if I'd be traveling with the computer and what the three main uses would be to determine how I would be using it and what would make it valuable to me. That salesperson showed more interest in me in sixty seconds than the other guy did in fifteen minutes. He was also genuinely interested in finding the right product for me rather than in making a sale. I told him that I'd been considering buying a particular model, and he promptly explained that the computer I was considering was more than I actually needed and that in the end I would spend more than necessary. His helpful advice increased my trust, putting him in the position to control the sale and keep me interested.

I wound up buying two laptops and a desktop computer from him in less than twenty minutes. Before I left, I asked him what else I might need and then purchased extra memory cards, software programs, and extended warranties. The first guy took fifteen minutes demonstrating his product knowledge, but he didn't bother to find out anything about me and he didn't get the sale. Why? He put product knowledge before people knowledge. The guy who sold me the product and got the commission also had plenty of product knowledge, and that was essential for him to guide me to the right product. But he didn't put the product knowledge first. He put me first. The human quality involved in selling can never be replaced, and it becomes even more beneficial the more deeply entrenched we become in the machine age.

I want to clarify: When I suggest you ask questions, it is not done with the intent of manipulation. This strategy has been greatly misused by sales trainers over the years. You are asking questions to find out more about how to help the human being in front of you rather than how to manipulate that person.

Many books on sales suggest a tactic of collecting information to use against the buyer later. They even describe tricks such as suggesting that the salesperson doesn't answer questions but that he responds to the buyer's questions with more questions. That is manipulation, not communication with the intent of helping the buyer, and it will not serve you over time.

I'm in the people business, not the product business, and I'm certainly not in the business of manipulation.

PEOPLE ARE SENIOR TO PRODUCTS (CRITICAL FOR EXECUTIVES)

Make this a fundamental rule you live and die by: You are in the people business, not the product business. People are senior to products! People are senior to processes employed by companies. No product or sales process will ever be successful if it doesn't make people senior! A product is dead; people are not. A process is a function and is always less important than people. To the degree that a company's sales process becomes more important than people, that process will fail.

A personal friend of mine who was a rookie commercial real estate agent asked me for a meeting about an investment property I was considering. I won't mention the name of the company he worked for, but I can tell you that it's one of the largest firms in the world representing apartment buildings, and it relies on a very stringent sales process.

I told my friend to come to my house for a meeting. He told me it was essential that I come into his office rather than him coming to see me. I thought this was strange and told him, "Just meet me at my office and let's figure out how I can buy something from you." He called me back and insisted that I come to his office! This was totally uncharacteristic of my friend. I asked him why he continued to insist on this, because there was no way I was going down to his office: If he wanted to meet with me, he'd have to come to my home or not meet with me at all. At this point he agreed. When he finally got to my home, we sat at my kitchen table and I asked him why he continued to insist that I come to his office. He explained that he'd been to a seminar and the company's sales approach *insisted* on the client going into the salesperson's office. This was a "control" point that the company promoted to its young salespeople, suggesting they would be able to control the client and get more listings.

While it's vital to have a sales process in place, the moment the process becomes senior to servicing the customer it will always err! This particular process failed to include me, the buyer! By the way, my friend never sold me any real estate. Instead, he quit his job at that company after I convinced him to come and work with me managing my property. This proved to be a very successful decision for both of us. He went on to become a prosperous business owner and real estate entrepreneur. To this day he thanks me for not meeting him at his office! People are senior to processes.

I remember when the Hummer H2 first came out. I was so excited after I'd seen one that I immediately called up a Hummer dealership because I wanted to buy one. I didn't need a Hummer, but I wanted one, and I wanted it now! A salesperson answered the phone and I asked how much a Hummer was. He told me that he couldn't give me a price over the phone. I asked if there was something wrong with him because I'd just called for a price, and he'd stated that he couldn't tell me. He said it was company policy not to give prices over the phone. Wow! What a policy. This Hummer dealership has a policy in place that prevents people from purchasing anything. He then told me that the policy was there to prevent people from shopping price over the phone and going to a competitor. I hadn't even been thinking about shopping a competitor until he planted the seed in my mind. *"Hmmm. Maybe I should shop the price. . . . "* I wondered why the Hummer dealership bothered to advertise its phone number if no one there was willing to answer questions.

This is a perfect example of a business that has implemented poor policy in an effort to prevent people from shopping competitors. Some genius in management came up with a policy that not only prevents people from buying, but also makes no sense to the buyer and probably no sense to the salesperson. This results in a complete waste of advertising dollars, creates a confrontational environment, destroys sales, and creates high employee turnover.

Processes put in place without considering the effect on the customer will inevitably be ineffective and destructive. People are always going to be more important than any processes, procedures, or policies.

People write checks; policies and processes don't. Products are dead matter and people are alive. Products can be replaced, but people can't. Products don't sell themselves, but people do. Never forget, people buy products, and it's your job to sell people on your product, not to sell your product to people.

Caring about people is senior to the products and the processes you use. Be genuinely concerned that your customer is getting the right product. Make the individual more important than the individual sale, and you'll make more sales. Be interested in what the person is trying to accomplish and what problem he's trying to solve, and treat people as individuals—as living, breathing individuals who are irreplaceable. Stay interested before the sale, during the sale, and after the sale—and even if you don't get the sale. Don't ever let the process be senior to the people!

You're not in the real estate business, mortgage business, insurance business, investing business, newspaper business, clothing business, acting business, hotel business, seminar business, or whatever "business" your industry calls itself. Quit the business you think you're in right now and get into the *people business!*

CHAPTER EIGHT QUESTIONS

While it is important to be an expert on your product, why is it more important to become a people expert?

What is the 80/20 Rule?

What are people most interested in?

What is the most important part of the definition of communication?

Write three examples of how to get someone to exchange communication with you:

1.

2.

3.

What one thing should always be kept senior to the product, policy, or process?

CHAPTER NINE

THE MAGIC OF AGREEMENT

ALWAYS AGREE WITH THE CUSTOMER

ALWAYS, ALWAYS, ALWAYS agree with the customer.

This is the single most important and the most commonly violated rule in all of selling! If you want agreement, you've got to be agreeable with your customers.

This vital rule must not be confused with the old saying, "The customer is always right," because customers aren't always right. If you've ever been with one, you know what I'm talking about. The point is, right or wrong, agree with the customer. Agree as you write the deal; don't disagree and fight the deal!

You can never expect someone to agree with you if you're disagreeing with him. It will almost never happen. People are attracted to products, ideas, and people that represent the things with which they're in agreement. This is a fact of the universe! Your friends are those people who most agree with your core beliefs. Your favorite family members are the people you want to spend your time with during the holidays. These are the people in your life with whom you've got the most agreement. People who agree with one another move toward one another, whereas people who disagree move apart. The common saying that "opposites attract" doesn't happen to be true in sales. In selling, likes attract, and like is born out of agreement. I like you because I agree with you at some level.

IT ONLY TAKES ONE

When there's not enough agreement between two parties, there's no agreement at all. This is the reason that partnerships fail, marriages break up, and you don't have more customers buying from you. Most people think that it takes two to have an agreement. But the truth is, it only takes one to agree, because once one opposing party agrees, there is no longer any disagreement. The salesperson who wants agreement must give agreement to the customer before agreement can be achieved. Even when a buyer is making ridiculous claims or exaggerations, agree with him. Just because you think what he's saying is ridiculous doesn't mean he thinks it's ridiculous. If he thinks something is black and you think it's white, you're both right. However, if he thinks something is black and you want to get the sale, you'd better agree with his reality that it's black. If he thinks he should wait and think about it and you disagree with him, you'll solidify his need to wait and never get him to close. However, if you simply agree with him that thinking about it is a good idea and let him know that you agree, he'll be more attracted to you and move toward you, not away from you. Once you've agreed with him, you can go ahead and explain that thinking will not change the fact that this is the right product, that he can afford the product, that his company will save money because of the product, and that by making a decision to buy it now he can shift his attention to all the other things he has to think about. Agree with him first, and that will bring him up to another way of thinking.

I wanted to add a fourth dog to our family and my wife was dead set against the idea. The first thing I did was agree with her. "You're right, honey. The last thing we need is another Great Dane."

With a raised eyebrow, she asked, "You agree with me?"

"Absolutely I agree," I professed. "You're right. There's no sense in us having four dogs."

That was the moment when she looked at the picture of the puppy and a little smile crossed her lips. "He is so cute."

Done! Dog number four is in the house! Do you get it? Agree, acknowledge, make the other party right, and then close the deal.

There is no single rule that salespeople violate more than this one, and it happens to be the number one rule in selling any product. AGREEING IS THE ROAD TO MORE SALES! This needs to be drilled and practiced because people are inclined to disagree in order to satisfy their gluttonous craving to be right.

THE AGREEMENT CHALLENGE

You have to really practice this, and it's best if you practice with a friend, family member, or work associate. You can even record different scenarios on a digital recorder and practice handling them whereby you agree first, then handle.

This is the drill: Try to agree with everyone you talk to for a single day. Try this around the house, as you're given endless opportunities every day to do the exact opposite of what I'm asking you to do in this drill. I'll bet you can't even make it through one day without violating this very vital and basic rule of selling. Try it! If you find yourself disagreeing outwardly with any person, then start over and keep at it until you can get through a whole day agreeing with everyone.

I know people who started this exercise at 8:00 a.m. and by 8:30 a.m. had already failed.

Your kid says he doesn't want to go to school today. Handle him by agreeing first. "I understand what you're saying because I didn't want to go to school on Fridays either. Now get dressed, my little buddy, and let's get to school."

Your husband wants to go see a new action movie, but you'd rather go out for a romantic dinner. Agree first. "You're right. It's a great night for a movie. Why don't we go down to that new café first and get a bite to eat?" Once you've agreed, it's possible to suggest alternatives that are more suitable for you. Now that you're at the café, you'll either learn to sell him on something else or you'll have to go to the action movie. Either way you are going to spend time with your spouse, and so both of you win.

A client tells you, "It's too much money." Now it's for real! "I agree it's a lot of money. Everyone who invests in this product agrees that this system is a big investment when they're buying it. That's why you should get it installed so it can start making you money right away."

"A new roof is a lot of money," the customer objects. "I agree it's a lot of money," you reply. "Your new roof is going to last for thirty years and there won't be any more leaks or costly repairs. You will have to do it sooner or later, so let's get it done now."

"The bedrooms are too small," the buyer says. "You're right," you agree. "That's one of the first things I noticed, too. What do you think can be done about it?"

Agree and then offer the buyer an opportunity to find the solution before you offer one to find out how much of an objection it actually is.

"We never make a rash decision!" the customer says. "And I agree with you," you say. "To make a rash decision would be the wrong thing to do, and I wouldn't want you to do that. However, you have been thinking about upgrading for some time now. You've used the same computer system for ten years and it's time to update it. If you would have done it nine years ago, it would have been rash, but now it just makes sense."

Agreeing with the customer is senior to all other rules in selling! Agreement is even senior to closing the deal. I can't believe I'm saying that because I see the close as something SACRED. However, if you disagree with someone before the close, you risk never getting to the point where you can close. Show me the top 1 percent of all salespeople in any industry and I'll show you people who are masters at agreeing with their customers first and closing them later on what they wanted all along.

Salespeople are constantly trying to sell and negotiate by disagreement. This is no different than trying to swim against the current. In most cases the person doesn't drown from water in his lungs, he drowns because he's exhausted from fighting against the water itself. Most salespeople drown in the negotiations from the exhaustion of trying to overcome every objection. Start the sale from a position of agreement, continue to agree, make the buyer right—close later.

You're right! I'm with you! I agree! Let me see what I can do for you! I understand! I will make that happen! Done!

Regardless of how off-key or incorrect the buyer may be, it's critical that the relationship is built on agreement if you want to make the sale.

Some people will say that agreeing when you don't really agree is manipulation. While I'm willing to agree with them that they see it as manipulation, I see agreeing as my attempt to get along. I think that disagreeing with people manipulates you out of a sale, and that doesn't make sense. If you say it's hot and I think it's cold, I'm able to agree with your *viewpoint* that you think it's hot. What have I lost? I'm simply acknowledging that you think it's hot. This is not manipulation; it's understanding. You didn't ask me what I thought. All I did was agree with your reality without adding that I think it's cold, which would only serve to make you wrong. By establishing basic agreement, you're creating the opportunity to help the buyer purchase your product or service. If the buyer never gets a chance to see what you're offering because of an earlier disagreement, then know that you've made an error by not allowing the buyer to see your product or service in the proper light. All you've done is put their focus on the disagreement rather than on your product.

HOW TO SOFTEN ANY BUYER

Let's say a customer tells you he's only got ten minutes and you know you can't do your presentation in ten minutes. I've watched salespeople spend ten minutes talking about how they can't do the presentation that quickly. A better alternative is to agree that ten minutes would be fine and go right into your presentation. If you start the relationship off with agreement, you'll have a chance to tell the prospect about your product. Additionally, you'll come across to the customer as understanding, easy to deal with, and professional.

I've been in hundreds of selling situations where the entire process started off with the buyer limiting the amount of time I had. I love this because I immediately tell them the time they offered me is more than enough. By the customer's response, you'd think I'd just stepped into a phone booth then flown out with a cape on. The buyer looks at me like I am SUPER SALESPERSON and immediately knows he's dealing with a professional. Customers respected me because of the fact that I agreed with them, not because I was slick at handling their objections. What created this response or change in the buyers? It wasn't some tricky, manipulative line. It was because I agreed to their limitations and I was willing to work with the amount of time they'd offered me. I showed them my appreciation instead of voicing disagreement. I'd rather have ten minutes than no minutes! By first agreeing with them, you can then move on with your presentation. Nothing will soften a buyer more than an agreeable salesperson.

THE MAGIC WORDS

Regardless of whether the customer is right or wrong, you need to make it safe for him to be right so he doesn't get so stuck in his "rightness" that he's unable to change his mind.

If you want people to agree with your viewpoint, all you've

got to do is agree with their position, agree with their opinions, and step into their shoes for a moment.

If you want to keep an argument going with someone, tell them that they're wrong. If you want to keep a raving maniac going on and on about how right he is, just disagree with him. If you want to get him to shut up, agree with him, and he'll stop behaving like a raving maniac.

There's no easier way to instantly end an argument than by agreeing with the opposition. A friend of mine who'd been married for seventeen years said that the magic formula to her relationship was telling her husband, "You're right." Who can argue with that? By ending silly arguments, one can move on and enjoy the important things in life.

Customer service problems can be handled the same way. When you get a complaint, go ahead and agree with the complaint. "You guys screwed everything up!" the customer shouts. "I agree with you, sir," you say. "Let me figure out how to correct it for you." But if you tell him he's wrong, you're only adding gasoline to his fire of disagreements.

You've probably experienced this phenomenon in your life. As an exercise, try it with your spouse or a friend. Wait until they say something and then tell them they're wrong. Watch what happens. You've just fueled an argument. To end the argument, tell them they're right! By agreeing, you cool off and put out the fire of disagreement. End of argument!

I once told a salesperson that I wanted to pay cash for the product, at which time he said, "You don't want to pay cash for it; you should finance it." His response created a block to my power of decision and lessened my enthusiasm for continuing to do business with him. By disagreeing with me, the salesperson created a barrier to what should have been an easy sale. He could have simply said, "Cash would be great, sir." Then, as he was taking my cash, he could have shown me both the cash price and the alternative if I financed, at which point I would have at least considered the alternative as a choice, not a "make wrong."

Agreement is the fastest route to getting your way! Do yourself a favor and practice agreeing with people. Three of the most powerful words in the English language are "YOU ARE RIGHT!" Two other powerful words in the English language are "I AGREE!"

Agreeing with the customer means control for the salesperson, happier customers, and quicker decisions. Miracles take place out of agreement.

CHAPTER NINE QUESTIONS

What is the first rule of selling?

How many people does it take to resolve a conflict?

To get an agreement, you must first do what?

Write responses to the following. (Then look at how I handled each comment.)

"It's too much money."

"A new roof is a lot of money."

"The bedrooms are too small."

"We never make rash decisions."

CHAPTER TEN
ESTABLISHING TRUST

SHOW, DON'T TELL

In this chapter, you'll discover how you can earn and secure full trust with your buyer and, in so doing, increase your effectiveness.

Because of a handful of unethical salespeople who have misrepresented the benefits of their products, customers may not completely trust everything you tell them. TV news broadcasts and papers are constantly running stories about scams and cons that make consumers skeptical of salespeople. This skepticism keeps the prospect on guard and prevents the salesperson from correctly establishing the trust that is critical to getting a decision.

Regardless of the cause, it's critical that you're aware of the buyer's lack of trust and that you tackle it. Distrust in the sales cycle is not the buyer's problem, but yours! If the buyer doesn't trust you or your presentation, the information that you're offering will be minimized, challenged, or shopped. Of course, the buyer will make a decision—it just won't be the one you want. When the buyer decides to "think about it," that's a decision, but unfortunately not the one you were looking for.

A salesperson always gets a decision from his customers. Always! They decided to think about it, and you got them to do that! You convinced them to go home and talk about it. They decided to present it to the board. That was all because of you!

When the buyer doesn't trust the salesperson or something about the presentation, he'll add time to the cycle by *not* making a decision to purchase. Even if you manage to close the deal, the unhandled element of distrust will almost always guarantee future problems in delivering and servicing the buyer.

When a salesperson understands what's going on in the mind of his customer, he's just stepped into an area that only a professional would delve into. The unspoken thoughts of the customer are an interesting field where you're no longer looking at what the buyer said; you're looking at what he *didn't say.* You're looking at what's going on behind the scenes in the customer's mind. When a salesperson is willing to go there, that's the point where he transitions from a painter to an artist! All my studies in sales over the last twenty-five years have involved the mind of the customer, not just his money.

PROSPECTS DON'T MAKE SALES—SALESPEOPLE DO

As stated earlier, prospects do not stop sales; the salesperson stops the sale. Understand also that prospects do not make sales, either. It is the salesperson's job to make the sale. Whether or not the sale happens is entirely up to the salesperson, not the prospect.

In order to make sales, you have to understand the mind of the customer. If you don't recognize how buyers think and what causes them to respond and act, you'll be unable to take full responsibility and will never reach your full potential. When you step into this arena, you are in the business of handling people, not products. People are run by their minds. Understand the mind and you understand people.

Most salespeople tend to blame their customers when sales are down, but they don't usually do so to the customer's face. They do it later when they're with their coworkers. "He can't make a decision. He doesn't know what he wants. He wants more than he can afford. He's just wasting my time." On and on! I never tolerate this sort of talk from any of the people who work with me. Such unwanted behavior is an indication of very low responsibility, and low responsibility = no sale.

The salesperson must assume responsibility for himself, the prospect, and all that occurs.

One time a buyer in a retail furniture store said to me, "I'm not buying anything today." With a smile I replied, "Sir, if you don't buy anything today it'll be my fault, not yours." He looked at me with a grin and said, "Great. Let me tell you what I'm looking for." The customer *did* buy from me that day and we furnished his entire house. All I did was take full responsibility for the selling *and the buying*. Also, I understood that his statement that he wasn't buying was just a reactive response from his mind and not really *him*. The only thing the buyer should ever have to do is give you the money.

The buyer who says, "I'm not buying today," is indicating his lack of trust of either salespeople or his ability to make good decisions. It's vital that you understand why the buyer is wary of salespeople and why he distrusts his own ability to make decisions. These points must be understood and handled.

When someone meets you and you sense his or her distrust, know that it doesn't have anything to do with you personally. You haven't even said anything yet! Perhaps the blue shirt you're wearing reminded him of some bad experience he had. I don't know, but I do know that if you don't handle it, you will not sell him!

CREDIBILITY = INCREASED SALES

A lack of trust will cost you sales! Distrust will cost you credibility, and lost credibility will add time and reduce your chances of making the sale.

Credibility is one of the most valuable assets you have as a salesperson. When something happens that calls your credibility into question, it becomes difficult to get the buyer to trust his decision to do business with you. If an element of distrust exists, no matter what you say or how you beg, plead, or persuade, realize that you've got your hands full and you must handle the distrust first in order to get the job done. You must rebuild your credibility immediately. Ignoring the credibility issue won't make it disappear. It has to be handled! When the buyer doesn't trust, you can use all of the greatest closing lines throughout history and watch them fall upon deaf ears.

Great salespeople understand the buyer's distrust, accept full responsibility for it, and never take it personally.

I always assume that the buyer doesn't trust a single word I say to him. He might not even believe that my name is what I say it is, which is why I create something that buyers know they can trust because they can see it. When I'm talking about the product, I provide everything I say in writing or support it with printed materials. If I'm telling a buyer that the piece of property is 44,000 square feet, I'll show him the documentation that supports my statement, and this will start to show the prospect that I'm trustworthy—that I know what I am doing. Then he'll lend credibility to what I say in the future!

PEOPLE BELIEVE WHAT THEY SEE, NOT WHAT THEY HEAR

Have you ever noticed that a buyer isn't fully listening to you? This phenomenon occurs because the buyer assumes that he can't trust what a salesperson says.

People believe what they see, not what they hear. Always have your presentation, proposals, and prices in writing for your buyers so they can see it with their own eyes.

Your prospects will not believe the words they hear, but they will believe the words they can see. Tell a guy some unbelievable and bizarre conspiracy theory that you heard about and then show him the article where you read it. If it's in writing, it becomes more real to him.

I had a very wealthy friend and I wanted to get him to invest with me on a real estate deal. I didn't tell him a single thing about the property, the deal, or the investment. I didn't waste one second telling him how good the investment was, since he had been told this a thousand times. I called him and asked him to meet me at the property because I wanted to get his opinion on how I could expand my company and wanted him to see what I was doing so he could give me the best advice. I *showed* him the properties, the tenants, the competition, the possibilities. Within thirty minutes of touring just one of the projects, he was asking if he could invest in the project!

I want you to make this a rule that you sell by: Assume that your buyer, no matter how well you know the person, never believes your words and will only believe that which you are able to show him.

As I stated earlier, there are many reasons for distrust, and it's necessary that you know what they are. The most common and least considered is the buyer's own experience with fabrications, exaggerations, and embellishments. You've got to assume that at some point in his life, he committed such an offense himself. It might be something major or it might be something minor, like the time he lied to his parents about not feeling good so he didn't have to go to school. Whatever it was, the buyer knows that another person is capable of slight exaggerations or even outright lies because *he's done so himself.* The buyer believes that if he's done this, you'll do it too, even if you won't! Regardless of how honest you are and how much integrity you might have, your prospect believes that you're capable of the same things he has been guilty of. This belief and distrust is what is real to that person, regardless of how much you try to convince him otherwise.

The element of distrust is intensified when your prospect has had the negative experience of being ripped off by some earlier salesperson or at some time when he had a plain misunderstanding between what was said and what was promised. People have misunderstandings all the time, and misunderstandings can lead to distrust. I want you to try this simple exercise to prove my point: Write down a short story about something that happened to you and read that story to one person. Then have that person pass it on verbally to another person. Continue this until at least five people have heard the story. Have the last person come back and tell you what he was told and compare it to what you wrote down. I assure you that your story will have changed. It didn't change because of lies, but because of incorrect duplication and misunderstandings. If you had passed your story in writing to each person, there would have been a greatly reduced chance of misunderstandings.

HOW TO HANDLE THE BUYER'S DISTRUST

The rule for handling a buyer's distrust is to always use and show written material to support your presentation and proposal. When you're documenting facts for your customer, it's preferable to use third-party materials that support what you're saying. Remember, people believe what they see, not what they hear.

Always, always, *always* write down what you've said, offered, proposed, promised, implied, and suggested. Anytime you're going for the close, insist on putting it in writing.

I see so many salespeople shying away from contracts, buyer's orders, and signatures! Why? Because they falsely believe that they may scare the customer with a pen or a contract. This is a ridiculous assumption that has no basis in reality.

You don't go into a military operation without equipment and supplies, and you never go for the close without a pen and a contract! There's nothing to hide. You aren't a covert operative or some kind of criminal who needs to sneak around. You are a professional salesperson offering a product that will benefit and solve problems for your prospects when they purchase and own it.

When you're presenting your product, write it down or show potential buyers the benefits on paper. If you're showing them how your product will improve their business, show them the proof by using statistics and success stories. I used to keep an evidence manual with me to show my facts and what others had said as a result of doing business with me. People love to see that you are prepared and sold on your product.

When you show your prospect what your competition will do or will not do, prove it in writing. When you know you've got the best price, the best product, and the best service, always back it up with documentation. If you do this satisfactorily, you'll earn trust and reduce the prospect's need to shop, think, research, and talk to others, all the while increasing your odds of closing the sale.

It's incredible how much significance people place on the written word. You want to capitalize on that. Every day, people quote things that they read in the paper without ever researching the facts for themselves. They assume that if it was written it must be true! People read books in school and then go through the rest of their lives believing that what was in the books was true. Twenty years ago a book was written and the first line read, "Life is difficult." This book became a best seller and everyone adopted this one line as truth, when it was garbage. That line certainly isn't true to me and it's definitely not a quote that I'd live my life by. But because it was written, people assumed it was true and adopted it as their own reality.

Newspapers perpetuate things that are not true and history books are filled with errors, opinions, false reports, agendas, and even outright lies. Some of the best-known books were written many years after the events even took place and long after all of the players were dead. Yet if it's written, people tend to believe it's true! Remember the movie *Jerry McGuire* where the character played by Cuba Gooding Jr. kept saying to the Tom Cruise character, "Show me the money!" In sales, the customer is Cuba screaming, "Show me the data!" That's the point here: Show the proof to the prospect, make it real to him, and he'll have the confidence to buy.

With the abundance of information available today through third parties, consumer guides, the Internet, and other sources, your prospect becomes even more dependent on facts to support decisions. Buyers are going to continue to rely on these sources, so you need to make use of the same sources to support your cause and help the buyer make the right decision.

Anytime you're presenting product information, performance reports, facts, historical data, comparison information, pricing data, proposals, etc., the rule is *don't tell, show.* The automotive industry is notorious for not wanting to give information to prospects, and because of this error, the industry suffers from high turnover, poor loyalty, high advertising costs, and shrinking profits. The premise was, "The less they know, the better off we are!" Nothing could be further from the truth. The more the buyers know, the more they can trust the information and the more likely they are to buy. By offering written information, you'll find that your sales will be easier, you'll make more money, and you'll have more satisfied customers.

As a salesperson, I prefer informed buyers over uninformed buyers for the very reason that an informed buyer can make a decision and can be handled with logic, while the uninformed buyer cannot make a decision and tends to get emotional. When facts, data, and logic are missing, people get emotional, and when people get emotional, they can get irrational. It's okay to sell with emotion, but you want to close with logic, data, and facts. An informed professional buyer is much easier to sell than one who is not informed. Someone who is not informed about the product will make an offer that has no reality to it. That would be an emotional offer, not a logical one. I want logic and facts in the close, not emotions. So I keep people logical by providing them with credible validation they can trust.

TIPS ON USING WRITTEN AND VISUAL INFORMATION TO CLOSE

- Never sell with words. Always show documentation.
- Never negotiate with words. Write your negotiations down on paper.
- Never ask for the close with words. Use a buyer's order.
- Never make verbal promises. Put all of your assurances in writing.
- The more data you provide, the better. Don't be afraid to use a lot of data.
- Keep your information current.
- Have your written information available and easy to access.
- Use third-party data as much as possible.
- The more you're able to access the data in real time, the better. Real-time data are preferable to prepared data.

- Use computer-generated data whenever possible.
- Have Internet access available so you can pull the data up in front of the customer and he can see that it hasn't been contrived or manipulated.

Make it easy for the buyers to do research while they're with you instead of at home or at their offices when you can't be there. If the buyers want to look up their own information or research, encourage them to do so.

After consulting with thousands of companies on improving their sales processes, I've often encouraged business, management, and salespeople to make all competitive advertising available and fully displayed in their offices so that the buyers don't have to go out and look at what the competition is offering; instead, they can do so without leaving.

HELP 'EM BELIEVE YOU

People want to believe you, but you have to help them. If you have a good product and a good service, then do everything you can to build your case and do it with written information. That way the buyer doesn't have to trust you. Once buyers read that what you're saying is so, they have no choice but to believe you.

I was involved in selling a 144-unit condo project that I owned, and the onsite management was having trouble selling the units. I decided to visit the building and find out what was going on. I walked into the office and asked them to run me through the process like I was a prospect. I found that there was no place to sign in and the pricing wasn't available because the pricing sheets were kept in another office. They weren't able to quote me a payment and finance rates and there were no data available to explain what the product offered. There was no competitive pricing displayed and there was nothing to offset the bad news about the neighborhood in the local newspapers.

I fired the project managers, installed a new group of inexperienced but eager people, and made sure that they had everything available for the sales team and prospects to look at. We sold thirty units in three months. That was three times the sales that the previous people had made in a year.

Some people distrust the selling profession because of the actions of a few criminals and the inactions of many well-intentioned salespeople who don't understand this basic rule of selling: *People believe what they see, not what they hear.* So show them, don't tell them!

CHAPTER TEN QUESTIONS

List three reasons people don't trust salespeople as suggested by the author.

1.

2.

3.

Whose problem is it to handle the customer's distrust?

When your prospect doesn't fully trust the salesperson or the presentation, what will he add to the cycle?

Give an example of when you didn't trust either the salesperson or the presentation and added time to the decision.

What is one of the most valuable assets of a salesperson?

The author suggests that people believe what they see, not what they hear. Explain.

What are four ways the author suggests building trust?
  1.
  2.
  3.
  4.

GIVE, GIVE, GIVE

THE MAGIC OF GIVE, GIVE, GIVE

Selling is the act of giving, not getting; serving, not selling. Unfortunately, most people in sales are looking for their commission and what they're going to get out of the deal rather than what they're going to give, what their product really offers, and how the client will benefit. The old adage is that it's better to give than to receive, but in selling, the only way to receive is to give first.

I believe that the true essence of selling is not just getting the sale, but the sincere desire to help. I also believe that a spiritually aware person will ultimately be a better salesperson than someone who's just interested in compensation.

I believe and have validated in my life that if you give enough in life, life will give back to you. It's the same in sales as it is in life. I don't mean giving the lowest price, or giving products and services away for free, but giving the most attention, the most energy, the best attitude, and the highest level of service.

Give, give, give is the assurance of sales, sales, sales. If your client wants one option, give him three, six, or even twelve options.

I created a software program for retailers based on the give, give, give philosophy. The program is called Epencil™ and provides the client with multiple options on different products in a succinct and professional manner. Epencil™ has been extremely successful in the auto industry where, for years, salespeople were inclined not to give information or to give only limited information. What I introduced was a program wherein a customer who asks for information is given an array of payments, package options, and price information, thereby making the buyer feel serviced, not sold. This concept of taking give, give, give to an actual application resulted in increased profits, increased sales, and happier customers for auto dealers. It fully utilizes the idea that service is senior to selling and giving is senior to getting.

If someone asks me for a drink, I get it for them, open the bottle, and bring them a glass, ice, and a napkin. That's give, give, give in action. I don't ask them if they want the glass and the ice—I deliver it and leave it to them as to whether they want it in the bottle or want me to pour it over ice! If I'm a waiter, I don't ask if you want dessert after dinner. I bring you the dessert tray, tell you about each dessert, tell you about my favorite, and dare you to pass. I can service you into the dessert without ever seeming to sell it!

A friend told me a story that illustrates the give, give, give attitude. She and her husband were leaving a restaurant in New Orleans one evening, and as they walked out onto the street, a haggard-looking man in a threadbare coat approached them. He immediately asked the husband for permission to serenade his wife. Reluctantly, the husband agreed and the man got down on his knees before her right on the sidewalk and began singing. She said that the incredible voice and heartfelt passion that came from that desperate character was powerful enough to blow the glass out of every window on the block. The man went on singing for two minutes, pouring his heart and soul into that song and giving them every fiber of his being. When he finished, they were speechless. Her husband handed the guy $100. With tears of gratitude, the man thanked them, then ran down the street to a beat-up car where his wife and children were waiting. The only thing that the guy had to offer was his voice, and he knew that if he didn't give it right then and there, his family wasn't going to eat that night. My friend's husband, a career salesman, said that he'd been so impressed by the man's intention to give that he hardly felt $100 was enough for what he received. That man on the street poured his soul into his song with the give, give, give attitude, not knowing if the couple would tip him at all. Regardless, for those two brief minutes, he belonged entirely and completely to them.

Give all of you to a prospect, not just a part of you. Give all of your attention, all of your energy, all of your suggestions, all of your information, and then find some more of you to give! Exceed expectations and go all the way with him and then a bit further. Withhold none of you and give yourself without reservation.

As a customer or client, I don't want to have to ask a salesperson for something. I want him to offer it. I want him to predict what I need and offer it to me. I want to be provided with what I ask for and everything else that will help me to make a decision.

This shows me that he wants to take care of me, is thinking like me, and is actually predicting my expectations and surpassing them all at the same time. Deal closed!

LOVE THE ONE YOU'RE WITH

Always pay attention to your customers and stay with them from start to finish without allowing interruptions. Show each customer how important they are to you and how they're the most important person in your universe. If you can do that you will be rewarded. If you chase two rabbits at the same time, both will get away. Commit to the one you're with all the way. Handle your phone calls and e-mails later and never allow interruptions.

Make your total commitment to that one opportunity, that one customer, and let him know that! Give your customers all of you and they'll see that you're with them all the way. Regardless of them taking calls, or you being interrupted, keep your focus on the person you're with. Too often, people feel neglected in life; so don't let them have that experience with you. Show them complete attention from beginning to end! Give, give, give your full, undivided attention to your customer and don't stop until you bring it home!

Make it your goal to give 100 percent of your attention to the customer regardless of the quality of the prospect or the estimated odds of closing the deal. Human beings are much more valuable than money. Treat them like that and you'll be rewarded.

In the business of sales, you have to be willing to serve people, not just sell them. For a business to survive and prosper it has to serve and help people, not just sell products. That means taking take care of customers and going beyond their expectations. The best salespeople I've ever met were not the fast-talking guys, but the most service-oriented ones. Those professionals who care the most are the ones who go the extra mile to find ways to improve the customer's life.

ARE YOU A HOLIDAY INN OR A RITZ-CARLTON?

As a salesperson, are you a Holiday Inn or a Ritz-Carlton? Be honest with yourself and you'll see why you're being paid whatever you're currently making. If most of your customers are grinding you on price, then your level of service is not obvious to them; otherwise they wouldn't grind you on just the price, because they would value the service you give them.

One time I had 1,700 apartments for sale. I had real estate agents lined up around the block begging for the listing, but none of them got it because I didn't trust that they would service me the way I wanted. I gave it to the guy that I knew and trusted, and I actually paid him double what I would have paid any other agency. I chose him because I truly believed that I could count on him to give me the best advice and the best service. The agent that I chose was someone I believed in, and I was willing to pay extra for it. Why would I do that? Because like most people, I don't want the best deal, I want the best service, the best product, and the best representation. I want to know that you're going to be there for me no matter what. I want to know that there's not going to be unnecessary drama and conflict, and if there is, I want to know that you'll handle it.

Selling is about helping people, not just selling them. If you like helping people and perfect the other points I'm suggesting to you here, you will be great. Many salespeople whom I've met, who otherwise could have been great salespeople, have unfortunately been corrupted by others who led them to believe that they should rely on trickery and deception. You don't have to trick or deceive to sell. You have to be willing to serve and help people before you'll get the close. The more you're able to demonstrate that service-oriented attitude, the easier your job will be. And trust me, no matter how much you serve someone you'll still have to be prepared to ask, "Will that be cash, check, or credit card?"

Service is the only way to higher prices and less competition. A salesperson caught in a constant price conflict will never agree with my point because he's stuck on price as the solution. But price is not the solution; it never has been and never will be. Service is the solution! A better product is not the solution because sooner or later someone will have similar or better products and will sell them at a lower price.

A buyer will pay extra for great service, a great attitude, ease of purchase, convenience, and being made to feel special. Look at how you can create a level of service that separates you from others. Going to the client rather than waiting for the client to come to you is service. Providing options is a way to service a customer. Sending gifts, flowers, notes, or just dropping by to say hello is service. A big smile, your full attention, and a great attitude are service. There's no real value in lower prices. What do I get for a lower price? I get a lower price and less service. I can get a room at a Holiday Inn for a fraction of the price of a room at the Ritz. What do I get for saving $400? I get a cheaper room, minimal service, and "I don't care" attitudes. What is the difference between a $500 room and an $80 room? Service!

You don't have to look far to find companies that are known for great service and higher prices. People even brag that they pay extra to do business with them. Look at Tiffany's, Ritz Hotels, the Four Seasons, and American Express Centurion. There are high-end beauty shops where haircuts are $700, but they aren't selling haircuts—they're giving service in abundance.

This kind of service is no different for a salesperson. If you elevate your level of service above the rest of the market, your customers will quit shopping the price. How much are you willing to bend over backward to make sure your customers are happy?

I once attended a seminar as a salesperson where the speaker said that one should never call and ask the client how the product was working because it opens the conversation to problems. While the audience agreed, I sat there in absolute disagreement. *If my customer is having a problem, then I want to know about it so I can handle it.* Problems and dissatisfaction are opportunities for me to shine, for me to separate myself and to sell again. It's not a service department's problem, it's my customer's problem, and I want to take care of it for him.

Tip: Problem = Opportunities for Future Sales.

SERVICE IS SENIOR TO SELLING

No amount of slick advertising or public relations can make up for poor service. Twice a year my wife and I go shopping for new clothes, and one time we decided to go to a big department store in our neighborhood that had recently started promoting a new image of personal service and customer satisfaction. After twenty minutes of walking around this store, not a single person had greeted us. Not even a hello! It was unbelievable. We were two qualified buyers with the intent to buy something and there was no one willing to help us or even acknowledge that we were there. What were these people thinking? I left that store feeling infuriated and swore I would never buy there again. I would never waste another minute of my time in that place. It would have been easier to steal the merchandise than to buy the merchandise there. When I got home, I opened the mail and what did I find? A slick invitation from that same department store inviting me to come down and shop its big sale!

Service is always senior to selling—always. One of the best people I know who is an example of high levels of service is my friend Gavin Potter. While I consider Gavin a friend, he sells me constantly on contributing money to projects for which he raises funds. I consider him a friend and not a salesperson because of the extraordinary service he gives me. He is an incredible salesperson, but beyond that, he's dedicated to high levels of service and thoroughly convinced of his cause. His commitment to his purpose alone and his dedication to high levels of service is what makes him great. One without the other results in mediocrity. Gavin has both barrels loaded: Service and purpose. I guarantee you that if Gavin were to run his statistics, he would find that his sales rise with every service-oriented action he performs. He knows that service is senior to the sale, and that's why he's in a league of his own as a salesperson.

If you incorporate these simple truths about giving and providing stellar service, I assure you that you'll become a master of your trade. You'll experience a confidence that you cannot put any value on, and that is worth more than money itself. You'll be able to name your price, go where you want, work with whomever you choose, sell whatever products you choose to sell, and provide for yourself and your family in ways that most people only dream of! You'll also experience a lifestyle that very few people actually have—one free of stress, worry, and problems. So give, give, give of yourself fully and provide unparalleled levels of service!

CHAPTER ELEVEN QUESTIONS

In your own words, what does the author mean when he writes, "Selling is about giving, not getting; servicing, not selling"?

What are four things you could give away other than the lowest price, products, or services?

1.

2.

3.

4.

Give four actual examples of how you give something without it costing you anything.

1.

2.

3.

4.

What does the author mean when he says you should love the one you're with?

What things would you have to improve immediately about yourself to be rated as a Ritz-Carlton?

1.

2.

3.

4.

What is the only way to higher prices and less competition?

CHAPTER TWELVE
HARD SELL

THE HARD SELL

It has been said that you have to ask someone five times before you get a yes. I don't know if that's true or not, but I do know that most people will not buy without someone asking them to, and people will never say yes to someone who quits asking. It has been my experience that the moment you quit asking, the deal is dead.

It's also been my experience that most people will not just give you the money without you asking, persisting, and being willing to "hard sell." I'm not talking about pressuring the buyer. I'm talking about being willing to get to that hard place in the close where everyone gets a little bit uncomfortable. The salesperson must be willing to stay in the deal and persist through to the close because he believes deep down inside that the product or service is right for the buyer. The salesperson must be willing to persist even when it gets hard, difficult, or uncomfortable. That's what I mean by "hard sell."

A buyer once told me, "Grant, you're pressuring me." To that I explained, "Sir, you're confusing my belief and passion in knowing this is the right product for you and your company with pressure. Please don't misinterpret my enthusiasm for pressure. Now, let's do this."

When you hit "hard sell" status, you've become convinced that your company or product is the only answer and any other choice would be a disservice. At the place of "hard sell," you're certain that your service is superior to that of anyone anywhere and ultimately the only right choice your customer can make, and you insist on it because of this belief. Because you believe this so deeply, you're willing to stay in the deal even when it gets uncomfortable and people are squirming, making excuses, and becoming difficult.

One of the best salespeople I've ever met is a woman named Charmaigne. She's a full-time fund-raiser and a dedicated master of her trade. Charmaigne isn't selling a tangible product; rather, she's raising money for charity to help people around the world. She called me up one night and asked for an appointment. I agreed, but made it clear that I wouldn't be making any more contributions as I'd already fulfilled my charitable donations for the year. "Yes, no problem," she said. "I just want to come over to see you and catch up." She came over and we talked for a while, and then she asked me to think about donating more. I adamantly told her, "No! Absolutely not! No way! I already told you that I'd donated all that I'm donating for the year. I am done, Charmaigne!" Unshaken by my outburst, she looked at me with a smile and said, "Now, Grant, the only reason you're acting like this is you know you haven't done enough." I couldn't believe her audacity to take everything I'd just said and handle me! Once the initial shock wore off, I started laughing and did what all people do when they're sold—I gave more. Charmaigne is dedicated to her cause, which is what makes her a master fund-raiser. She could have been "polite" and left when I started hollering at her and things got uncomfortable. But she didn't. She stayed and she got the close. The willingness to stay and persist even when the prospect becomes noisy is what separates the professional, consistent closer from the amateur who randomly closes deals.

If you don't truly believe that your product will somehow bring the buyer more enjoyment, benefit, or security than the numbers he has in the bank, then you'll never be a great salesperson and you'll never fully understand the concept of "hard sell." If you really believe and learn how to close, you'll know someday what it means to hard sell. This is an art form!

THE FORMULA FOR HARD SELL

There are only two things that can get you to the point of being a true professional hard-sell closer:

1. You must believe that what you're offering is the right thing for the prospect.
2. You must be trained to stay in the close *no matter what happens.* You'll need to be armed with an arsenal of ways to handle stalls, emotional reactions, and objections. My closing program is vital for arming you with the technology to master the hard sell. Go to www.GrantCardone.com or call 800-368-5771.

CLOSING IS LIKE A RECIPE

There's no way around the fact that you have to know what to say and it has to sound natural. Does this mean you need to become rote in your responses and have some formulated way to handle a specific objection? Absolutely! It's like a recipe. It takes certain ingredients combined in a certain order and put into the oven at a certain temperature for a certain amount of time. Do it exactly per the recipe and you get what you anticipated; change one thing and you don't. The more you practice handling objections, the more natural you'll sound. It's like the grandmother who makes fudge without even looking at the recipe. She has done it so many times over the years that she doesn't need to read over the list of ingredients anymore. She just knows what to do—and her fudge comes out perfect every time. It's the same thing with handling objections and closing deals. There's nothing wrong with learning what you're going to say and how you'll handle certain situations.

If you were giving a press conference to the world, you'd drill and practice what you were going to say. You'd consider how your address would be perceived and the effect that it might create before you'd go out in front of the world with it. You have to do the same thing to prepare yourself to become a professional hard-sell closer.

You need to practice handling objections and stalls so that you can persist intelligently through resistance. I practiced this daily for years. Every morning I'd team up with another salesperson and we'd practice every possible situation we could possibly encounter that day. That training turned me into a lethal individual at closing deals. If you can't close, you lose.

I've done this in many different industries, only to find out that all objections are similar and the closing techniques cross over from one industry to the next. If you can't persist with closes due to the fact that you run out of material, then you'll never reach the hard-sell level! If you don't learn how to hard sell, you won't make it to the level of the greats!

I suggested to you earlier to work out how you're going to handle situations. I don't want you looking shocked or surprised or having to run off somewhere to figure out what to do. I don't want you going home to think about what you could have done differently—leave all that to the amateurs. To be a professional and get professional results, you have to know what you'll do and say in every situation.

Videotape yourself and perfect your techniques. I recorded myself every day and watched my gestures, my hand motions, and even my emotional responses. Throughout the day I'd write down all of the objections I heard, and the next day I'd team up with another associate and we'd practice handling them until I was satisfied. Drill and practice build confidence. You're already doing this now, whether you know it or not, but you're doing it to build bad habits, not good ones.

STANDING IS FOR LOSING, SITTING IS FOR CLOSING

I've watched salespeople enter negotiations standing up, which is a common error. They stand there talking about their prices, payment plans, programs, guarantees, and benefits, and in so doing, they're only talking and not showing. No wonder they aren't closing! They're talking too much and not using anything to establish their credibility. Remember, your buyer will believe what he sees, not what he hears! Talking and telling aren't closing. They won't get a salesperson even a remote shot at the close!

You'll almost never close a deal if you're standing up. Sit your clients down and show them what you can do for them. Support it with facts they can see and substantiate. Standing up is for walking; sitting down is for closing. So sit your customer down and get your buyer in a position to be closed. *"Sit right here, sir, and let me SHOW you the facts about the product."* Don't pitch it; show it. When you're making a proposal, sit the buyer down and write down the facts and figures. Telling him verbally is a waste of time and effort and almost never results in a close. So sit the buyer down and show him what you've got, and be prepared to hard sell in order to close the deal.

CHAPTER TWELVE QUESTIONS

How is "hard selling" someone different from pressuring someone into buying?

What is a great way to handle someone that suggests you are pressuring them?

What are the two things you have to become convinced about in order to reach hard-sell status?

1.

2.

What is the formula for hard sell?

1.

2.

What are the three suggestions the author makes for learning how to hard sell?

1.

2.

3.

CHAPTER THIRTEEN
MASSIVE ACTION

TAKE MASSIVE ACTION

Most people incorrectly estimate the amount of effort it takes to get the results they want. When it comes to taking action, never think in terms of balance; always think in terms of massive amounts of action. Assume in the case of action that more is better and less is nothing. Whatever you think you need to do to get the job done, increase the amount far more than you think is necessary, and you'll get results beyond your wildest expectations.

Never let the psychiatrist types convince you with their psychobabble and mumbo jumbo that you need "balance" in your life or that you should "stop pushing yourself" and "live in the moment." This advice is promulgated by those who apparently want you to have a mediocre life, and they have no evidence to substantiate this advice as valuable. The more I work and accomplish, the better I feel. The less I do, the more tired I feel. When it comes to getting big results and becoming wildly successful, you have to take action in that direction in massive quantities. There's no way around it.

I love action, and the more, the better! I love getting things done, and I bet you do, too! I love the satisfaction of accomplishing a task. I'm happiest when I'm producing and creating. I love working in my yard more than I like lying on my sofa.

If you want to get anyplace in life, you've got to take action. If you want to take a trip, you've got to fill the tank with fuel and then accelerate the car down the highway. If you want to build a house, you've got to pound nails and pour concrete. If you want to win the lottery, you've got to buy a ticket. To get results, you have to take action! The amount of success you have is limited by the amount of action you take. Stay away from the people who tell you to stop working so hard and suggest that you should relax and take it easy. You can take it easy once you make it. For now, take action, and take it in massive quantities.

I took massive action in my life and have done so until it became a way of life, a discipline. Am I a maniac? I certainly don't think so, and I can tell you that I'm living a life that no one in my entire heritage has ever experienced. Do you think a man gets elected president of the United States without taking massive action to ensure he gets elected? Do you think Tiger Woods didn't take massive action to become the greatest golfer in the world? Mr. Woods out-practices everyone in his field, and because of this dedication to massive action, he has reached levels that others never dreamed of. To become president in your field, you will have to be out of balance, totally focused, and dedicated, following up with tremendous amounts of action.

THE FOUR KINDS OF ACTION

You can never take enough action in life; you can only take too little. Too much action will never get you into trouble. In fact, taking action is the way to get *out of trouble.* The only time action will cause you trouble is when there isn't any or when there's not enough of it.

It's been said that there are three kinds of action in life:

1. The right action
2. The wrong action
3. No action (which will always result in nothing)

And in my world there's a fourth kind of action:

4. Massive action! That's the one I live by!

The fourth kind of action, massive action, is by far the most successful tool I've had in my life. It has resulted in more success for me than anything else I've done. When someone asks me what one thing has made the most difference in my life, this is it—massive action. Even when I had no clue what I was doing, I went ahead and took massive action. If I wanted to get a loan on a piece of property, I always went to three or four lenders. When I bought a piece of property, I made bids on more than one property. When I throw a party, I invite lots of people and then repeat the invitations. When I'm done with invites, I get on the phone and I keep calling until I'm guaranteed a great party. I don't like small parties. I like them big and noisy with lots of people. I'd rather have too many than too few. Once I had a party at my home and went through 2,500 plastic cups! Now that's the sign of a real party! I didn't even know half of the people who were there. You've heard the saying "Go big or go home"? I say "Go massive, not passive!"

MASSIVE ACTION = NEW PROBLEMS

I watch salespeople make a few phone calls, send out a few pieces of mail, and then stop to take a coffee break and gossip about the latest news in the local paper. Then they sit down and chatter about how business is slow and how the phone and prospecting don't get them results.

If you worked the phone the way I do, you'd know that the phone does not work; it's the person *on* the phone who's working. I never sit down to make one phone call. Never! When I sit down to use the phone, I do it with enough tenacity and with such massive quantity that I'm guaranteed to get something in return from my actions.

If it's appointments you want, take massive action until your concern is no longer whether or not you'll get enough appointments, but how you can possibly handle all of the appointments you have. The right amount of massive action should result in new problems.

One of my goals in my seminar business is to sell out the locations to the point that there aren't enough chairs to seat the attendees. This goal always worries my sales guys because they don't want the customers to get upset about not having a chair after they've paid $800 for a ticket. That's a new and good problem to have! One of my salespeople protested that it wasn't fair to the audience. I said, "Bring it on, ding-dong! You fill the place up to the point where people don't have a place to sit and I'll handle the fallout." Never worry about the wrong things; if you do, you won't ever get what you want. Doing too much will never fail you, but doing too little always will.

When it comes to action, go big, go bold, and then go more. This is the *one thing* that will guarantee results. Don't deal in small numbers and small actions. Deal in large numbers and massive volumes of action. Go massive, not passive.

When I was a young salesperson, I was rough around the edges (my wife says I still am). But I never let that stop me from taking action. When you're not perfect and polished, the only way to compensate is by taking lots of action. You'll find that when you get enough volume going, you don't have to be perfect. You'll never become polished at this career if you've got only a handful of opportunities. The more action you take, the more business you'll have, and the better you'll get at your job.

If you're unlucky enough to be one of those polished and professional types, you'll still need to take massive action in order to get to the higher levels of production. I say "unlucky" because I've met many veteran salespeople who have been around for years and are very professional and know their business, but have an air about them that says they're superior to others and don't have to keep learning and changing and taking action. Wake up! It takes massive action, not polish, to get what you want in life! No one will pay you for what you know. They'll pay you for what you do.

PRODUCTION YIELDS HAPPINESS

Most people don't get enough in life only because they never do enough in life! Production makes people feel good. It almost doesn't matter what you're producing as long as you're doing and producing something constructive. Decide to produce something and produce it in massive quantities, and you will win in life. Production results in happiness. This is a basic truth in every religious, economic, and ethnic group on this planet. People feel better when they are producing, and the more production they generate, the better they will feel. Money may not make people happy, but production will. In the words of Dr. Michael DeBakey, "Man was born to work hard."

In sales, massive action is the one single thing that will guarantee you increased success more than any other! If you want to guarantee X, take massive amounts of action that will achieve X in abundance. Your problem will no longer be how to achieve an abundance of X; rather, it will be how to manage the abundance of X.

Massive Action = New Problems. It's at this point that you know you're doing enough.

Throw a pebble in a pond and it creates ever-widening ripples. Pound the pond with mortar round after mortar round and then follow up with more mortar rounds, and you'll create a massive lake. Everyone around will come to see what you're doing.

By taking enough massive action, something will be changed, something will be created, and results will be attained. In the sales arena, massive action is like the stairway to heaven, where the sales gods will praise you with trophies, trips, rewards, and the guarantee of new levels of income! Your fellow salespeople, however, may praise you only with criticism, tell you that you're working too hard, and give you free advice like "Slow down—smell the roses." Disregard them and consider their suppressive comments to be a sign that you are on the right track. Just continue to add wood to your fire. All fire requires constant fuel, and success in sales requires more action.

Anyone who tells you that you're working too hard is not working hard enough. Unfortunately, such people have given up their hope of having an extraordinary life. Such people are mediocre at best and have forgotten about the dreams they used to have. Take massive action until you get new problems, at which point you will get new levels of sales results. Don't quit until you get new problems—problems like taxes, cars, homes, and where to go on vacation.

THE 10X RULE

If you want one thing, take massive action equal to at least *ten times* what you think it will take to ensure that you attain that one thing. If you do that, you won't have to hope, wish, cross your fingers, or pray for what you want. What you want—and far more—will come to you when the right amount of action is created!

A salesperson once told me about the bad luck he'd been experiencing. His appointment canceled, a buyer backed out, another customer had to change his order, and so on. I told him that his problem wasn't bad luck or misfortune; it was that he didn't have enough in his pipeline. I suggested that if he took ten times more action than he had been doing, he would have no time to dwell on these so-called misfortunes and would have actually welcomed someone canceling out, as it would have been a relief rather than a misfortune.

If you take enough action and are getting results, then it's no big deal when an appointment cancels or a buyer backs out. In fact, you'll welcome the occasional cancellation since it'll increase your ability to get to everyone on your lineup. But if you're taking only small amounts of action, every time you lose a deal, all of your attention is diverted to the so-called misfortune and the loss because you don't have anything to replace it with. You've put too much attention on too little. Put your attention on massive to ensure that you don't become passive.

ACT LIKE A MADMAN

An associate of mine watched me call a client fifteen times in three days without the client ever returning my call. Was that too much? I don't think so. When I want to get something done, I keep taking action until I get what I want. Never be reasonable when it comes to taking action. Just take more action. Be almost insane with how much action you take to get the job done.

A farmer should plant far more than he can possibly eat so that if a drought or famine occurs he can still take care of his family and his neighbors. A realtor who wants listings should call hundreds of people to get just one and will probably end up with many. If you want appointments, call every friend you have and every past client. Stop people on the streets if that's what it takes. Be mad in how much action you take until it becomes a habit, a way of life, and normal for you. Once you are greatly successful, people will talk about how successful they always knew you would be, rather than how crazy you were. In no time, you'll be overflowing with appointments, sales, and success.

Act like a madman when it comes to action and get completely unreasonable about what you think it will take to get the job done. Be without sanity or logic or reason when it comes to taking massive amounts of action and you'll reach heights that others never dreamed possible. Massive action first equals new problems, but then will equal massive sales.

CHAPTER THIRTEEN QUESTIONS

What is the one thing the author states that most people incorrectly estimate in order to get the results they want?

Write down a time when you underestimated the amount of effort that was required in order to reach a goal and how much you underestimated the effort.

What are the four kinds of action?
1.
2.
3.
4.

What will a person immediately experience from taking massive action?

The author says that most people never get enough in life because . . . (finish the statement.)

What is the 10X Rule?

CHAPTER FOURTEEN

THE POWER BASE

WORK YOUR POWER BASE

Salespeople tend to put their attention on selling to people that they don't know and ignoring the people they do know. Entire companies advertise to people they don't know and to whom they haven't sold. They even advertise to people who are not even interested in their products. Salespeople wait for people they don't know and even call people they don't know, while completely ignoring their known lines of influence. This is one of the most violated basics that salespeople overlook in their careers.

Everyone has a base of power in their life where things are familiar and known. Typically, it starts with one's family and friends. Most everyone has a place where there are elements of understanding, comprehension, safety, security, and strength. The easiest sale you'll ever make in your life is the one to those people who already know you, trust you, and want to help you. Everyone has a power base or a fan club. Don't ignore it; work it, use it, and mine it like gold.

Your power base is made up of the people who will be happy to hear from you and want to know what you're up to. One of the fastest ways to not get into power in your career is to abandon those who love you, care for you, and have some interest in your life. Therefore, no one has to start from scratch in building a base. Everyone knows someone.

I had a customer who had bought many products from me, and we became personal friends. I called him up one day and I told him, "Get over here right now. I have to show you something." He asked me what I was up to and I repeated, "Just get over here as soon as you can." Not long after he showed up at my office, I pulled out the buyer's order and told him to sign it. He asked, "Sign it? But I don't even know what I'm buying." I assured him, "Don't worry about it. I would never mislead you and I guarantee that you're going to want this." He signed the order, I presented him with his product, and he fell in love with it! It was that simple. I sold him something he wasn't in the market for and didn't know he needed, and it was one of the easiest sales of my life. You can do things like that with your power base. Think of yourself as the center of the base, and the closer to the center of the base the individual is, the easier the sale.

HOW TO BUILD YOUR POWER BASE

The first thing you need to do is make a list of your power base. Your power base includes, but is not limited to, friends, family members, associates at past jobs, past employers, current and former clients, members of clubs, neighbors, members of orga-nizations you belong to, members of your church, and believe it or not, even people who didn't like you in high school.

Who are they, where are they, how do you contact them, and what should you say? What you say to them is the easiest part. Just tell them what you're doing. First make your list and then make contact. Let them know what you're up to and find out when you can meet with them to catch up. The purpose of the meeting is not to sell them; that will happen naturally. The purpose is to get in contact with them and to work on restoring your power base.

If you've come up with a list of ten people, automatically con-sider that number to be at least one hundred. Each of the people you know will have at least ten people in their own power base who can benefit from what you're selling or the service that you're offering. If you don't believe this is true, then I suggest you go back and reread Chapter Five in this book and resell yourself on what you're doing.

You can contact these people by phone, in person, by mail, or by e-mail. The best way is to meet face-to-face if possible, so drop in or call and set up a time to have lunch. Don't worry if you haven't seen these people for years. Forget the past. Go catch up with them and create your future. Take interest in your con-tacts and mine your power base. Find out about them—what they're doing, their work, their family, and everything that's going on. Restore the relationships. When it comes around to you, let them know what you're doing and how much you love it. You can broach the subject that you'd love to show them your product, but at this point your intention is simply to restore, rebuild, and mine your power base.

IMPOSE ON THEM OR HELP THEM?

People want to help people that they know. Put away any reservations that you have and contact them. Get rid of that silly idea that you'll be imposing on the relationship. That's ridiculous. What are friends and family for if you can't impose on them so you can help them? Someone is going to sell them—why not you? The reality is, they want to help you as well. If you love your product and fully believe in it, then love your power base enough to let them know what you've got. Rely on the earlier rule about taking massive action and use it on your powerbase. Contact enough people in your powerbase, and someone will tell you that they need your product or service. If you have a problem about imposing, you're really having a problem on being sold and you need to get back your commitment.

From there you can expand your list.

Let's say I sell clothes and I have ten friends, each of whom has a use for the kind of clothing I'm selling. Each of those people has an average of 2.2 more people in their household. That's twenty-two people, expanded from ten.

Let those first twenty-two people know what you do, what you sell, where you are, and how they can contact you. Get their addresses and put them on a mailing list. Collect their birthdays, or if you want, just send out random birthday cards. No birthday card is better responded to than one that's been sent out on the wrong day. Everyone will call you informing you that you have the wrong date for their birthday, at which point you'll say, "I know that, but I didn't know what your actual birthday was, and I thought I'd just take a chance at being right!" I guarantee you they'll call. You have to get creative about contacting people. A little imagination combined with massive action goes a long way. Don't ever worry about making a mistake. The only mistake you can make is failing to make contact.

Get these twenty-two people to help you meet the people they know so you can start working that list. Work the power base from the inside out and watch how big it gets.

When you're making your power base list, you're going to be shocked at all the people you've forgotten. Don't worry about it; just go on and make contact! They'll be glad to hear from you and want to help you.

I once contacted a guy from high school that I used to get into fights with when we were teenagers. I called him up and told him that even though twenty years had passed, I still thought about him often and had laughed at how we'd been enemies. Not long after that, he came into my office and bought my product from me. Speaking from experience, I can tell you that it's easier to sell a past enemy than it is to sell someone you've never met. Don't deny your power base. Work it!

If *you* don't help your power base, a guy like me will. All of us have had the experience of running into an old friend who owns a product that we represent but who bought it from a competitor. The competition had worked the prospect, and you lost a sale because you simply failed to contact your power base.

The worst part about making a sale is that you just lost your best prospect and now need to replace him! The new customer now becomes part of your power base. Ask any salesperson anywhere, "Would you rather sell someone that you've never met or someone that you've sold to before?" If you were to poll a million salespeople with that question, all would agree that they'd rather sell to someone to whom they've already sold. Why? Because they have the experience of winning with that customer, and that makes it easier to sell the person again. The relationship is there, trust is there, and an experience is there. This is your power base now getting bigger. Add this to the enlarging circle that is emanating from you, and stay in contact with these people.

CAPITALIZE ON THE EASY SALE

Existing customers are the easiest sale to make, and I always prefer them over a brand-new prospect. I know what turns them on; I have a relationship; I have their trust; and they know me, the company, and the products I represent! Even when an existing customer has a complaint or a problem, that's just a great opportunity to turn the complaint or problem into another sale.

I have a policy in my office that all complaints are to be immediately brought to me. Why would I want to deal with complaints? Because I know that complaints are one of the most overlooked opportunities for additional sales. Problems are opportunities! Solve the problem and you gain an even better customer.

Another reason that former customers are easier to sell is because it's easier for them to make a decision with someone they've done business with before. People are creatures of habit. When I do a sales seminar, 99 percent of the people who attend choose to sit next to someone they know. Why? People find comfort in familiarity.

CREATING POWER!

Most salespeople don't capitalize on familiarity enough. I like doing business with people that I know. I like it that you already know what I like, what I want, and how to talk to me. I like it that you already know what my expectations are and how I want to be serviced. I like it that we have an experience that we survived together. But I wonder if the salesperson feels the same way; after all, he rarely calls me after he sells me.

Do you not think I'll buy another suit, another computer, another cell phone, television, house, appliance, car, another piece of property, or make another investment? Do you think I'm done because I already played with you once? Do you think I ran out of money or that this was the last time any human being would close me on a similar product? Do you think that you captured the entire amount of my credit limit? Always remember, you won't be the person who sells the customer for the last time. The question is, will you sell him the next time? I can assure you that if you don't stay in touch with your power base, including your previous customers, you'll never attain power in your business. Never neglect your former customers!

If you want to guarantee certainty in your sales production and ensure yourself a long and happy career in selling, stay in touch with the people in your power base. Love them, call them, wine and dine them, send them presents, and continue to show interest in them.

I bought my first real estate investment from a friend. He'd been told by his mentor after months of working with me that I would never buy anything from him and that he was wasting his time with me. I bought forty-eight units, and the following month I bought another thirty-eight. So much for the mentor with the great advice. But the story doesn't stop there. This guy became my partner and quit the firm he was working for to manage the property that I had bought from him. He thought I was done after these first two purchases and quit aggressively looking to buy more. I would call him to say I was looking for more deals, and he would be pessimistic about the prices and my probable ability to purchase more. Another long-term friend of mine, Dale, happened to be in my office after I'd hung up with my new partner in frustration. Dale asked if I would give him the same deal as I gave my other partner if he found me some deals. I told him yes, and shortly thereafter I started working with him on opportunities. Over the next two years, I bought another 400 units, and then another 1,500 after that.

My first partner is a great guy and did very well for himself, but he violated his power base. My old friend Dale made millions off the deal by staying close to his power base and working it. By the way, Dale had no experience in real estate and the first guy did. He was flat broke at the time we hooked up—fifty-two years old with less than sixty dollars to his name. Today he's a multimillionaire. That's a true story. Dale saw the opportunity to work his own power base and he grabbed it. The moral of the story is to stay in touch with the people in your power base.

Keep as much attention on the people you just sold as you do on the people that you want to sell next. And build power from your power base!

CHAPTER FOURTEEN QUESTIONS

What does the author suggest is one of the most violated basics people overlook when trying to sell their ideas or products?

Make a list of ten people in your power base.

1.
2.
3.
4.
5.
6.
7.
8.
9.
10.

What is the worst part of making a sale?

What is one of the most overlooked opportunities for making additional sales?

What does the author suggest are the five reasons that an existing or past customer is an easier sale than someone you don't know?

1.

2.

3.

4.

5.

TIME

HOW MUCH TIME DO YOU HAVE?

The most powerful man in the world has 24 hours in a day to get done what he needs to get done. The richest man in the world has 3,600 minutes in a day to earn his money. The most educated man in the world has 168 hours in a week to learn. The greatest athlete in the world has 365 days in a year to train. How much time do you have?

When people tell me that they don't have enough time to do what they need to get done, I don't believe it. I recently read that the average person in this country watches three hours of television a day, which translates into 67,500 minutes a year. Do you realize how many phone calls you could make in a year with that much time? If every call lasted only three minutes, you could make an extra 22,500 phone calls a year. That would be 1,875 calls a month. 75 calls a day! If you did only a portion of that you would reach the top half of the top 1 percent of all the salespeople in your industry.

It's actually a *lie* when you tell yourself that you don't have enough time! The fact is, you have the same amount of time as everyone else; you just aren't using it efficiently. We all have the same 24-hour days, amounting to 8,760 hours a year. If you don't know how much time is available, I assure you that you haven't decided how to use it. If you agree that time is money, then you should inventory and protect your time just like you would anything that is valuable.

I had to travel to Las Vegas recently for a speaking engagement. As my driver dropped me off at the airport, he asked when I'd be coming home so he could arrange to pick me up. I told him I'd be arriving the following day before noon. He then suggested, "Why don't you enjoy yourself and spend an extra night and come back the next morning?" I replied, "Rather than wasting time in Vegas and making them richer, I'll come home and get back to work and maybe make myself richer. Who knows? Maybe by being home and being in the office I'll close the biggest deal of my life." "Ahh," he said, "that's why you're where you are and I'm driving you." Exactly! And that's how you will get where you want to go—by maximizing every minute of every day. Anyone can be where they are now. The question is, can you get to the next place? Only by using time wisely.

USE EVERY MOMENT TO SELL

When I'd been selling for a couple of years, a man named Ray took me under his wing because he saw some promise in me. He pulled me aside one day and asked, "Grant, why do you go to lunch with your fellow salesperson Gene so often?" I was perplexed by the question because it seemed perfectly natural that I'd go to lunch with my friend and coworker. When I wasn't able to answer, Ray looked at me and said, "Grant, Gene will never buy anything from you. Never!"

Wow! What he said fell on me like a truckload of gold bricks, and it really got me to confront how much time, energy, and money I'd wasted by going to lunch with Gene. As I thought about it, I realized I'd been wasting one hour every day, six times a week, for 52 weeks of the year. I'd spent 312 hours of my time with no opportunity whatsoever at making a sale! I never went to lunch with Gene again after that, and my sales began to pick up. I made it a firm policy that if I wasn't eating with clients or potential clients, I'd eat lunch in my office while I called clients.

HOW MUCH TIME ARE YOU WASTING?

Starting today, I want you to take a look at how much time you waste in a day. Every time you find yourself doing something that is not productive, make note of it. Smoking, taking coffee breaks, standing in line, calling friends or family, gossiping, standing around the water cooler, discussing the game, going to bars, doodling, daydreaming, avoiding work, etc. Write it down and become aware of all the things you're doing that don't add up to moving your team and your company down the field. What if you had only one hour to win the game? You can't take breaks when you've got to work the ball down the field. You have only three one-minute time-outs and you're on the clock. When the buzzer rings, the game is over!

He who makes the most of his time will accomplish the most.

Make the decision now that you're controlling time—and time is no longer controlling you. Change your mind about time and decide that you have plenty of it. Become a master of the clock, not a slave to it.

THE LUNCH OPPORTUNITY

A partner and I were at a lunch meeting with a group of potential clients. The group seated my partner and me together, so I requested that we be seated at different tables. Why? Because I can't sell my partner and there is no opportunity in sitting next to him! The goal was to be with as many of these clients as possible, not to be with each other. I sat at one table and he sat at another, thus doubling our exposure.

I learned this valuable lesson back when I was a salesperson wasting lunches with my coworker Gene. Today I won't go to lunch with a fellow salesperson, a manager, or even the boss. I need to spend time with customers. Going to lunch with your boss will not get you job security, but selling more products will. My rule is if they work with me, they won't buy from me, and so that excludes them from spending lunch with me. You need to work your sales career the way a politician works his campaign. He doesn't keep talking to the people who are already going to vote for him. He goes and talks to the people who haven't yet decided who to vote for.

Today I invest breakfast, lunchtime, and dinner with buyers, prospects, and even long shots. These lunch dates would include anyone who might someday buy from me. Even when I'm not taking a customer to lunch, I'll frequent places where I've got a shot at being seen, where lots of people go, or where I might just luck out and run into someone who will buy from me.

People who go out for lunch are typically qualified buyers. They're working: Bankers, insurance people, salespeople, entrepreneurs, etc. These are the buyers of your products. Go out and be with them, be seen by them, and get to know them. Find a restaurant where qualified people go to eat and show up there every day until you get to know the scene. Visit that one place and become known there before moving on to other locations. Get to know the owner and the waitresses until they know you by your first name. Then you'll get to know the patrons. Go to the places where potential customers congregate at lunch and be seen by them. Personally, I like to go to the pricier restaurants because they attract the better-quality customers. Aristotle Onassis, the great shipping magnate, always made a point of going to the most expensive restaurants throughout his travels when he was a young man. Not because he could afford it, but because the people there had money, and he wanted to be around opportunity and success.

I once made a sale to an insurance agent and offered to buy him lunch as a sign of my appreciation. I met him at his office, where we loaded up his wife and daughter and went off to his favorite place. At the time, I was thinking small and was worried about how much the bill was going to be. Within five minutes of sitting down, he'd already introduced me to a friend of his at another table. My client's intro was, "Vic, this is the kid I was telling you about," at which time Vic pulls out a card and says, "I want one just like he got. Can you have it at my office today?"

LUNCH OUT = SALES UP!

That brown bag lunch you made to save yourself $10 will cost you hundreds of thousands of dollars in lost sales. Go out, be seen, mix it up, and put yourself in the game. Use your lunchtime to meet clients and don't waste this opportunity by hanging out with friends and other employees. You can't save your way to being a millionaire, but you can certainly sell your way there! Quit trying to save money and start doing whatever it takes to be seen, to get noticed, and to make sales!

My wife is an actress here in Hollywood, and I asked her where the best place is for people in her business to be seen. She told me that the place to be seen is at the Ivy. Well, guess where we go to lunch now? People remember who they see and forget who they don't see. Some people even take it as a "sign" when they see you that they should do something with you.

Lunch is about business and opportunity. It's not about food, friends, and family. Lunch is an occasion to create contacts and show appreciation for past customers! Utilize it and work this one-hour gold mine. Make the most of every day by knocking out the wasted time and cleverly scheduling your valuable time! Some people might wonder if there's ever any time to just relax and take it easy. Sure there is, but that comes later, after you've reached your goals and made your dreams come true.

If you aren't where you want to be in life, you've got to work every minute and snatch up every opportunity. You owe it to yourself, your family, and your future. Make every moment count!

CHAPTER FIFTEEN QUESTIONS

How much time do you have? Don't look.

Write down six activities that you consider to be a waste of time for you and how much time you think you waste on each activity per week.

1.
2.
3.
4.
5.
6.

Multiply each of the above by 52 and then by 20 to calculate the cost of each activity to you every year in time and money.

1.
2.
3.
4.
5.
6.

Write down the two activities that make you the most money and how much time you spend on them each week.

1.
2.

CHAPTER SIXTEEN
ATTITUDE

A GREAT ATTITUDE IS WORTH MORE THAN A GREAT PRODUCT

People will pay more for an agreeable, positive, and enjoyable experience than they will for a great product. Who doesn't want to feel good? Who doesn't want to be acknowledged for being right? Who doesn't want to be smiled at and agreed with? Show me a person that doesn't want to feel good and I'll show you someone that you don't want to bother selling! People want to feel good. People are moved by positive and confident people, more than by great products. There will always be a market for products that make people feel good, but a person who can make someone feel good can sell almost anything! The individual who combines a great attitude with a great product becomes unstoppable!

A positive attitude is a thousand times more important than the product itself. Just observe how people on this planet spend their money. A person will spend a small amount of his income on the necessities of life and blow his entire paycheck on entertainment. Why? Because he wants to feel good! Why does Jay Leno make more money than all of the schoolteachers in Los Angeles combined? Because he makes people laugh and feel good.

It's easy for a buyer to say no to a product or a company, but it's extremely difficult to say no to a positive experience with another human being. When something makes you feel good, you want more of it, whether it makes sense or not. This is why people do things that aren't good for them, because for a moment or two, it made them feel good. People will spend money on things that make them feel good before they'll spend money on things they need. This explains the poverty and debt levels we see today.

Once I saw a beautiful jacket on display in a shop window and was so intrigued by it that I went inside to have a closer look. I asked the clerk the price, which she told me as she helped me slip the jacket on. Admiring my reflection in the mirror, I protested that the price was insane and added that I didn't even need the thing! With a warm, understanding, and beautiful smile, she said, "No one buys a jacket like this because they need it. They buy it because it's beautiful and it makes them feel good." Melting in the truth of her statement, I asked her, "Do you take AMEX?"

With all the chaos and bad news that the media disseminate daily, it's refreshing to meet a solution-oriented, positive person. You know the kind of person I'm talking about. The kind of person who's always smiling as he says, "Yes, sir, I'll get it done for you. I'd be happy to do that!" I want to be taken care of by positive people. I don't want to just be sold. I want people around me who are positive, helpful, smiling, and motivated. That's what all people want.

I have a personal assistant named Jen. When I hired her, she had no experience with the type of businesses I own and had never worked in the kind of environment we have. I didn't hire Jen because of her abilities and experience, but because of her positive attitude. Jen is an upbeat "can-do," get-it-done-with-a-smile-on-her-face kind of a person. That doesn't mean she doesn't make mistakes; she does. But because of her attitude, the mistakes are acceptable. I never get mad at her no matter what she does because she's so service-oriented, so positive, so "Yes, sir, I'd be happy to do that for you." Is Jen selling? Absolutely! Every day, whether she knows it or not.

Never let anyone convince you that people won't pay more for a great attitude and great service. The ability to be positive at all times, whether you're winning or losing, is the one thing that will ensure you're a winner in the end. Attitude is senior to it all! I love positive people and find them irresistible. When you are positive, people will find *you* irresistible.

TREAT 'EM LIKE MILLIONAIRES

My wife and I often go to a place called The Grove for dinner and a movie. We valet-park the car there, and this bleached-blond, spiky-haired guy always greets us, opens the car door, and smiles like he's glad to see us. "Good to see you again, boss," he says. "Leave it with me. I'll see you in a couple of hours and your car will be right up front." He gets a $20 tip from me every time, even though I could have parked the car myself for $2. The other valet guy who works there greets us like we're a nuisance, doesn't smile, appears to hate his job, and parks the car in the same spot that the spiky-haired guy does. Due to his poor attitude, I give him $5, and that's only because he parked my car for me. I'm sure he then goes home and tells his girlfriend how cheap all the people are who valet their big cars and that his spiky-haired partner is just luckier than he is.

It ain't the luck of the spiky-haired guy, I assure you, and it is definitely not that I'm a poor tipper. It's the attitude that makes the difference. The reality is, people with good attitudes are luckier than people with bad attitudes. There is no treasure greater than a great attitude and no way to get real treasures without having a great attitude!

A customer wanted to buy a truck from me one time, and like many car buyers, he didn't want the dealership to make any money off the deal. He thought it was fair that he pay only invoice for the truck. None of this makes any sense, of course, because if the company sells its products for invoice then it won't be able to stay in business to service the customer.

But because I know that attitude is more important than the product or the price and because I trusted that the customer would pay for my positive, can-do attitude, I told him, "No problem, whatever you want, it's yours, my friend. I just appreciate having the opportunity to do business with you." He was shocked at my response and the smile I had on my face because I hadn't let him get under my skin. I spent the next hour or so with him, showing him the truck, getting to know him, laughing with him, and being a positive influence on him. I treated that customer as if he were about to give me $1 million. I put aside the fact that he didn't want to pay above invoice for the product and pushed everything in the direction of a great attitude.

At the close, I showed him the documented invoice price on the truck, with state taxes of $4,000, and added another $2,000 for me to take care of him for the next four years. He looked at me and said, "I know I can buy this down the street without paying the extra $2,000." With a smile, I responded, "You're probably right, but you won't get me down the street." He laughed and said, "I don't know why I'm doing this, but let's do it," and he wrote the check.

Remember that a product can be shopped, but a great attitude cannot. A price can be beat, but a great attitude is priceless. There's nothing more valuable to anyone than a positive person.

People will always act according to your attitude. If it's negative, expect a negative response. When it's positive, you can expect a positive response. If I scream and threaten another person, you can expect him to flee or fight. Neither response is good for a salesperson. But if I'm positive and agreeable, I can expect the buyer's response to be the same if I'm contagious enough! When you have the ability to change people's attitudes in a positive way and make them feel better than they did before meeting you, you'll no longer need to rely on your product being superior!

How you act toward others will be how they'll act toward you. Your attitude precedes everything that happens to you in life. If you think about car wrecks, you'll have car wrecks. If you hang around with negative people, you'll start to get negative. Hang around people with problems and you'll attract problems.

A PRODUCT OF YOUR ENVIRONMENT

My mom told me as a kid, "You are the people you hang around with." While I resisted her wisdom at that time, I know now that it's true. Today I would take that great statement even further and say, "You are a product of all that you surround yourself with!" That includes the TV you watch, the newspapers you read, the friends you have, the movies you go to, your hobbies, your interests, your family, and everything else that you are involved with.

Every winter season the newspeople spend hours each day convincing you and your family that the flu season is coming, that you're susceptible, and that millions of people will get the flu. They used to call them epidemics, and now they call them pandemics. Do I think that people actually get the flu because it's promoted with such dedication? Absolutely! The media get everyone thinking about the flu, worrying about the flu, talking about the flu, and people will start to think they're getting the flu until finally they do get it!

When the media start promoting recessions and tough times, people everywhere tighten up, and this perpetuates exactly what was promoted. Entire economies can be frozen by what is promoted on television and in newspapers! The attitudes of entire nations of people can be shifted from positive to negative in order to influence the actions of many so that just a few benefit. The newspapers and television have been used for years to influence the attitudes and actions of the many. If the actions of millions of people can be altered by the news, certainly your attitude can influence one other person for the good or the bad.

Even the "medical profession" agrees that most mental and physical diseases are actually psychosomatic (of the mind). This has been proved with placebo pills that in many cases result in as much healing as those who took the real medicine. Even though the placebos are nothing but sugar pills, people believe they will help them, and so they do.

I believe that the single most valuable asset I have in my life is my ability to stay positive when everyone else is losing their minds. When everyone around me is freaking out and worrying and singing the blues, I choose to stay positive. By staying positive, you become the obvious leader, and people will follow your lead. If that position in life is desirable to you, then you need to do everything possible to protect your attitude from things that bring you down. You'll also need to take a preventive step and guard yourself against other people who may have the agenda of affecting you negatively.

It is not enough just to be positive; you have to actually protect yourself against those who are being negative. Watch out for friends, family, work associates, and others around you who have an agenda of negatively affecting those around them. Attitudes, like diseases, are contagious. Your enemies are not your problem when it comes to attitude; the problem is the people closest to you. Would you let your best friend leave his garbage in your house? Of course not! But that's exactly what he's doing when he comes over and starts telling you bad news, gossip, and all his troubles. You're allowing him to leave his mental trash in your environment, and you become infected.

TIPS FOR HAVING A GREAT ATTITUDE

If you aren't getting paid the way you want to and you know what you're doing, I assure you that your attitude is part of your problem! If you want a bigger paycheck, get a bigger attitude. The questions to ask are, how do you change it?; how do you stay positive?; and what can you do to ensure that you're smiling, happy, and loving life?

Here are some helpful suggestions that I've used in my life when I wanted to make sure I had a beaming, positive attitude.

1. Avoid newspapers, television, and radio.
2. Stay away from "can't do" people, people who have trouble in life, and people who don't do well. You can try to help people, but don't hang around with them and be affected negatively. This includes family and friends.
3. Get everyone in your life on the same page with where you're going and what you want in your life, as well as what's expected of them in order for you to get there!
4. Avoid drugs and alcohol because of the negative influence they have on your mind. They make you lethargic, slow, and unsure! Prescription drugs affect the mind as badly as the street drugs do, and some are proving to be even more dangerous. Just look at the side effects and warning labels. Control your attitude by being aware and alert, not by being drugged and numbed.
5. Avoid hospitals and doctors if at all possible. Go see them when you absolutely have to, but that's it. I've seen too many people get worse after they spend time with doctors and hospitals. Hospitals appear to be "sick factories" rather than places that heal people. Just watch people as they leave.

6. Treat negative talk like garbage. Put up a sign in your home and your office that reads, NO-NEGATIVE-TALK ZONE. Don't allow people to talk negatively around you. You don't need it. Treat it like garbage and don't allow anyone to leave their garbage in your environment.

7. Start the negativity diet today. Commit to no negative thoughts, ideas, or talk for the next twenty-four hours. This will be a start to you really getting control of your thoughts and actions, and it will help you build discipline to control how you think and act. Thoughts come before actions, and your actions then determine your life. Once you get control of how you think, you will then get control of your actions. The negativity diet works like this: No negative thoughts, talk, or actions for a full twenty-four hours or you restart the clock. While this may seem like a very simple challenge, I have never met anyone who made it through the first twenty-four hours without having to restart the clock, and I know thousands of people who failed the challenge only ten minutes after starting.

This is going to give you a game to play whereby you are competing with yourself to start controlling how you think, act, and live life! People have become unaware of just how negative they are, and then they wonder why they get negative results in life! Control your thoughts, and you will control your actions. This simple game will first make you aware. Once aware, a person can start making changes. Be gently honest with yourself while playing this game. When you fail, become aware of the negative thought or action, write it down, and restart the clock. Keep doing this until you are able to make it for twenty-four hours. Then see how many days you can go. The goal is to create awareness and discipline in what you choose to think and do in your life!

If you want to know how to permanently get rid of negativity, call my office and my staff will introduce you to the only guaranteed, surefire way to rid yourself of all your negative computations, ideas, and reactive responses and become the positive, forward-looking, solution-oriented person that you are supposed to be. The reality is, if you didn't have any negativity going on in the first place, you wouldn't need the negativity diet. Call 800-368-5771, and my office will turn you on to the most exciting adventure of your life.

Nothing in your life will pay you more rewards than your ability to have and maintain a great attitude. Nothing will prove more valuable in life than a positive outlook. People will remember you not for how much money you made or for your success, but for how you handled life and how you made others feel. Your attitude and your ability to have a positive influence on the attitudes of others will affect not only your sales, but every area of your life: Your marriage, your kids, your health, your wealth, your luck—*everything*. You name it, and a great attitude will affect it!

CHAPTER SIXTEEN QUESTIONS

What three things does the author state that people will pay for?

1.

2.

3.

What two things will make you unstoppable?

1.

2.

What are three ways you can treat people like millionaires?

1.

2.

3.

What does the author suggest is your single most valuable asset?

What are four tips for improving your attitude?

1.

2.

3.

4.

CHAPTER SEVENTEEN

THE BIGGEST SALE
OF MY LIFE

The first moment I saw Elena, I knew I'd found the girl I was going to marry. I was absolutely and completely sold from the first moment I saw her. It also became almost immediately apparent that she, like many customers I have had, wasn't going to make this sale very easy for me. I was taken aback by her beauty even to the point of being insecure about my qualifications to have her and my ability to get her attention. I pushed through my fears and introduced myself to her as my heart skipped and my pulse raced. She responded to me with complete disinterest, as though she couldn't even see me. You would have thought I was a ghost or that I was the invisible man. I was devastated, certain by her response that this sale would be almost impossible. The whole encounter lasted maybe a minute before she continued on with what she was doing and left me to be by myself.

I went to one of the people on the set—a friend (working my

power base)—and found out everything he knew about her and got him to give me her phone number. He was reluctant to do so, but he could see I was never going to leave without getting a way to contact her (hard sell). I called her the following day with enthusiasm and my great attitude, convincing myself that I could get her interested in me (attitude is senior to product). Again, it didn't go the way I was hoping: She still seemed completely uninterested in my product (me) and was a bit annoyed that I'd called her. I knew I was missing the mark, but I was totally convinced that she was the one (completely sold on the product).

I was unable to really get in communication with her because I didn't know what she liked or had an interest in. I was getting nowhere fast, but I refused to give up. Looking for some positive support and reassurance, I called my mom and announced that I'd met the girl I was going to marry. My mom was excited and asked if we'd been out yet. I told her that there was just one little problem: The girl had no interest in me. My mom, wanting to protect her son from being hurt, offered her advice on this situation, stating, "Grant, it takes two for a relationship. If she isn't interested in you, then you can't impose yourself on her." (Protect yourself from negative information—Be careful where you get advice when you are going after your dreams and goals; even the people who love you the most can offer information that could possibly cause you to get off the path of your dreams.)

The moment my mother said, "*It takes two,*" it hit me what I had to do. If the sale was meant to be, it was up to me! I've heard salespeople blame the customer for years for sales they didn't make. I immediately became even more determined to make this relationship happen.

If someone was to be sold it was up to me, not to Elena. If I waited for her to make it happen, it never would, so I had to get creative. Buyers don't buy until someone sells! And it doesn't take two, it only takes one. I decided at that moment that I would be the one to take complete responsibility for selling myself to her and closing the deal. What to do first: Get sold on the product again (me). So I sat down and wrote all the things that I had to offer and all the quality points that I would bring to the relationship. I then came up with an action plan. I started calling anyone who might know her and put it out there that I was interested in her and wanted to make it known (massive action). Then I decided to call her every few weeks until I was able to finally break through to her and really get into communication, with her giving me the chance to get to know her and her to get to know me. I called her monthly for an entire year, leaving nice little positive messages. Not only did she not take any of my calls, but she never returned a single one of them. But that didn't stop me, as no real salesperson will stop because of a little rejection. I just stayed interested and kept letting my interest be known. I was unreasonable and disregarded any logic. Since the phone calls were not getting any traction, I continued, when necessary, to remind myself that my product was good and my mission was great!

I went back to working my power base. I discovered, through persistence, that a friend of mine had a friend who was actually a girlfriend of Elena's. I then started by getting to know the girlfriend, and I told her that I was interested in Elena and updated her on my efforts and my lack of success (power base). I asked her to put in a good word for me and to find out what the deal was with Elena and why she wasn't responding to me. The girlfriend actually told me that Elena had mentioned my name before, saying there was this guy who kept calling and leaving funny messages, but that she didn't have any interest.

The girlfriend said that she told Elena I was a really good guy and that she should go out with me. As the girlfriend told me this, I got so excited, thinking, *I'm going to pull this off*, at which point the girlfriend tried to let me down gently, saying that Elena had stated that I just wasn't her type.

Is that a complaint or an objection? I wondered. What is the objection? I had to pull it out of the girlfriend, because I had to know what I was dealing with. I got Elena's girlfriend to tell me because I had to know (be committed). She finally told me that Elena had said that I was too short, that she didn't like businessmen, and that I just wasn't her type.

But those aren't real reasons not to go out with me—*they're just complaints*, I thought (know the difference between complaints and objections).

While all common sense was telling me to give up, I was walking down the street and saw this ugly guy with this beautiful girl and I thought, *How did he do that?* I didn't know the answer, but I knew it wasn't because he quit. So I decided I wouldn't quit until I at least got an appointment, sold the product (me), and went for the close!

I had to agree with her first, as that's the number one rule in selling. So I called her and left another message on her recorder, probably my thirteenth by now. "Hey, Elena, this is Grant. As you probably know, I've been bugging Erica about you. Look, I don't want you to think I'm a stalker or anything. I'm just a guy that's really interested in you and I have no intention of giving up until

you give me a chance. By the way, just as an update—I'm growing." I always kept the messages positive and upbeat and never
made her feel wrong.

One day I was asking a buddy of mine about Elena—he also
had been trying to date her. He told me she wasn't really interested in a relationship, but was more into shooting guns and her
career as an actress. He was actually giving me reasons why she
wasn't much of a catch (sounds like a salesman that couldn't close
a deal). I then pursued this information regarding shooting and
found out that Elena was one of the top ten women clay shooters in the state of California, and that shooting was her passion.
I called the L.A. Gun Club, rented the shooting range, and hired
the best coach in Los Angeles for the following Saturday. I then
called her again and left another message on her recorder telling
her that I had booked the club and the trainers and was asking
her out for a day of shooting. (Find out what they are interested
in, not what you are interested in.) Sixty seconds later, she called
me back for the first time! We had our first real encounter that
Saturday, and we were married less than a year later.

My wife was the toughest sale I'd ever made, and I can tell you
it was worth it. I have been in deals as large as $80 million, but it
didn't even compare to getting this girl to first pay attention to me
and then go out with me, and later being able to propose to her
and know she would say yes.

My wife will tell you today that I saw us long before she did
and that my conviction and complete knowingness of us as a couple were very difficult to resist. She will not say that I imposed or
pressured or stalked her. She'll tell you that I predicted the future
and created it by knowing what I wanted, staying with it, and

continuing to do whatever was necessary to get the deal done. My wife would not say that I sold her in some negative context but rather that I showed my love for her and put it all out there, regardless of her response to me (Give-Give-Give).

I will tell you that the most important sale of my life was this sale, and also that if it were not for my view of selling as a needed skill in life and an understanding of it technically, I would not have been able to get this worthy close.

SUMMARY

Your ability to persuade others determines by itself how well you will do in all areas of your life. Selling is an absolute necessity for really living life and making your dreams come true. While selling is a career for many, it's a requirement for all. You need to sell, negotiate, and persuade others in life to get what you want. How well you can do that will determine what kind of life you will have and how many people you can influence.

Become a student of this thing called selling. Don't treat it like something distasteful that you have to do or that you'll hire others to do. Selling is the ultimate fuel of every economy in the world. Without people selling ideas, concepts, and products, the world would never improve. If you want to make a difference on this planet, learn how to sell. If you want to make sure your worthy ideas get known to the world, you'll have to sell. If you want your way in life, if you want your company to do well, if you want your family to prosper, learn the information in this book, and I guarantee that you will prosper in ways other people considered impossible.

CHAPTER SEVENTEEN QUESTION

Write an essay about what you learned from this chapter and from this book so far, and describe how you are going to apply that in order to get what you want in life.

CHAPTER EIGHTEEN
THE PERFECT SALES PROCESS

In this chapter, I want to briefly introduce you to what a successful sales process looks like. First, it would satisfy all parties involved and increase the effectiveness of the user.

For fifty years, there has been very little change in how people sell things. Most of the information is dated, with encouragement to control your customers and spend long periods of time with them, believing the longer you spend with them the more indebted they become. The reality is that people have changed over the past fifty years. Wives are making more of the decisions about what is bought and how money is spent; both husbands and wives are now more likely to be employed; people have less time; there is access to more information; and some studies suggest entire generational changes whereby the buyer doesn't want to even engage a human being when making a purchase.

The perfect sales process then would have to be fast and easy for the buyer; easy and effective for the salesperson; provide credible information as easily as the buyer can access it himself; treat the buyer as an informed person, knowing he has access to knowledge; and ultimately satisfy the customer and the company by consummating a sale.

The first thing I would look at in any sales process is how to shorten and simplify it, just because of the amount of sensitivity buyers demonstrate to time. Whether filling up the car; checking out a gym membership; or shopping for an outfit, groceries, or technology, time is on your buyer's mind. How long will I be here? How long will it take? Am I going to get stuck with a person I don't want to spend time with?

Basically, the sales process is finding out the following about the buyer: Who are you? What do you want? Why do you want it? What do I have that will fulfill your wants and needs? How do I show it to you so that you can make sense of it; make an offer that can be funded; and then close, deliver, and follow up in the hope to repeat the process with you and others? Anything I can get rid of for the sake of speed and simplicity, I will.

The other thing is that the perfect sales process could be advertised. If you can't advertise any part of what you are doing, then there is something not OK with it. The transparency of the process is a vital litmus test for how much integrity your process has in it. The old adage was control, deceive, and withhold information, all of which would fail the test of being able to advertise the process.

Much of what I have been taught over the past twenty-five years I could not tell the customer because there was always something not OK with it. This is why I believe there is a disdain for sales. But it doesn't have to be like that. The best salespeople I know are straight shooters. They don't play games, they tell it like it is, and they know how to get the job done without manipulations and tricks.

The best sales processes are shorter rather than longer. Ideally, the salesperson is sensitive to the client's time, willing to spend as much time as necessary but never interested in wasting time. The buyer would be able to get in and out as quickly as necessary or spend as much time as needed to get comfortable enough to make a decision. Whether the buyer is coming to you or you are going to him, regardless of whether it is a very complex sale or very simple one, no matter the price or the terms, there are some things you must do and some you cannot avoid.

To determine if your current selling process could be problematic for your clients, ask these three questions: (1) Do you experience lower-than-average profits per transaction? (2) Is the length of time to contract the source of customer complaints? (3) Are you getting customers resisting your process?

Organizations are always looking for new salespeople, but what they should look at first is a new, shorter, more customer-friendly, matter-of-fact, information-focused, twenty-first-century sales process. Sales processes should be built to satisfy the following in this order: (1) Customer, (2) salesperson, (3) management (last).

Most selling programs were designed to satisfy what management wants, but in reality, management isn't buying the product and in most cases isn't selling it. An example of an old adage and belief in selling that would no longer apply today is, "The longer you spend with the customer, the better chances you have of selling him." This is no longer reality, in fact, the longer you spend with them the more likely you are wasting everyone's time.

If the process you are using cannot pass the first two hurdles of satisfying the customer and the salesperson, it won't be effective for management no matter how much management wants it, because it will be resisted. It doesn't matter how much I like my 750-pound Harley Davidson Road King or want my daughter to learn how to drive it, she can't operate the bike because it's too heavy for her. The point is that it doesn't matter how much the owner or upper management wants something done a certain way; if it doesn't work for the customer and the user is unable to execute, it will fail everyone!

The litmus test for a great sales process is the question, "Can we advertise to the public what we want our people to do?" If you can't answer yes to that, there is something wrong with your selling process.

I have worked with sales organizations and individuals around the world, and the following is what I believe to be a very powerful and succinct selling process. While it must be customized for you depending on your product or service, the basic format of it will prove effective. These are the shortest number of steps in order to simplify the process, remove waste of time, and still focus on the most important things you want to accomplish. Many organizations have ten to twelve steps, most of which are skipped, and many of them are resisted. Here are the most crucial five steps that you must encounter in every sales situation, whether it be in person, on the phone, or over the Internet:

1. Greet
2. Determine Wants and Needs
3. Select Product and Present/Build Value
4. Make Proposal
5. Close the Transaction or Buyer Exits

STEP ONE: GREET

The goal of the greeting is to introduce yourself, make a good impression, and put the buyer at ease. My goal here is to set the stage for the remaining steps. Say "Welcome" if they are coming to you and "Thanks for seeing me" if you are going to them. In both cases you should be interested in time. If you don't yet have a relationship with the client, you don't want to waste his time or yours trying to make a great impression of who you are and what you represent. If you do know the person, you don't want to get caught up in small talk and never get around to business. It is impossible to get rid of this step. What we want to do is use it to open the door to the reason we are there: To move the prospect into a buyer.

Examples of Greetings

- "Welcome. Thank you for coming here. What can I get you information on?" (Then transition into the remaining four steps.)
- "Hello. Thanks for taking the time to see me today. Tell me,

what homework have you done thus far so I don't duplicate your efforts?"

- "Great to see you today, and thanks for your time. What information can I provide you with to make the best use of your time?"

Each of these greetings gets to what people want to do. We save rapport building and buddy making for later in the process when and if the buyer elects to do so. (Call our office to get more information on customized greetings for you and your organization.) After each greeting, I immediately transition to step 2.

STEP TWO: DETERMINE WANTS AND NEEDS

Determine wants and needs and why. You can either do this by moving into fact finding or into a consultation stage. The fastest way to do this is to fact find on previous like purchases. The purpose of this step is twofold: (1) To know what product to show your client and (2) to know how to present the product in a manner that will build value in that presentation and cause the person to want to act.

Even things of equal value are not identical when the motivation for that thing changes. A glass of water is a glass of water, and on the surface would appear to be the same until you discover reason or motivation someone might want for the glass of water. Different reasons promote different values and urgencies, and those must be determined in step 2.

A glass of water just to finish the dinner table out has a different connotation than a glass of water that would be used to wash poison out of someone's eye or one to be used to satisfy the thirst of someone who is dehydrated. Furthermore, a glass of water from the local water system holds different value than bottled water or an alkaline water that is used to reduce the acidity of someone's body chemistry.

At Thanksgiving, the glass and aesthetic value of the presentation is more valuable than the water itself until one of the guests is choking on Grandma's cornbread dressing; then the same water increases in value and the glass diminishes in value. Get it? Why do you want this? Why do you have interest now? What is your current situation? What problem are you trying to solve? What is important to you in your next purchase? Why? What similar experiences have you had? What does your current situation do for you that you like? What does it not do for you? How would you rate your current service on a scale from one to ten? What would make it a ten? Would you do that again? Was it worth the money you paid? What value would you place on it? What would have made it better?

When determining wants and needs, you are not selling; you are asking and listening. Because this is done in the early stages of the sales process, understand that you will be using this information to make sense of and close on your proposal.

Remember, all purchases or investments are trying to solve a problem of some sort. All of them. You don't buy a drill because you want a drill. You buy a drill because you want a hole.

STEP THREE: SELECT PRODUCT AND PRESENT/BUILD VALUE

Select the product and present it. Select for your clients rather than allowing them to wander through your inventory and select for themselves. Whether your product is tangible or not does not matter; you have an inventory. If you're selling insurance, based on what you found out in the first two steps, you would now be able to select and present a solution and how it will benefit the client. The same holds true with any other presentation, whether it be surgery, a piece of art, a car, furniture, a membership at the country club, or a gift for a charity event—or a simple glass of water.

You should present your product based on what your client told you was important. There is no reason to show the quality of the crystal or quality of the water to a choking man. If I buy a home from you, please show me what I want to see rather than what is in my budget. And when you show me a home, if you have done step 2 right, let me see the property before you show me the house. When I buy property, I am more interested in the grounds than I am in the house itself. But if you don't take the time to find out in step 2 what is important, you will waste time in your presentation showing me things that just don't matter.

On my show, *Turnaround King*, you saw me go to a gym where they presented their products to me without knowing what was of value to me. Had the owner of the company taken the time to collect the right information and then presented his product specifically to me, he would have been more effective. Once he found out that the wet part of the facility was most important to me, not the weights and socializing, then he could have spent his time targeting his demonstration to those things that most hit my hot buttons. The fact that I love to swim and believe that swimming in an Olympic pool would trim me out faster than any other workout, without causing damage to my body, would have allowed the presenter to target and confine his presentation to those things that would have created urgency and the most value, and it would have improved his chances of making a new member.

Just because your client calls you about a property you have listed that has an 11,000 square-foot house on five rolling acres doesn't mean he needs to see all 11,000 square feet or under every leaf and blade of grass. In fact, you won't know what to show the client until you ask. Then, in your presentation, focus on those things that are most important to that buyer. Shorten your demonstration process to laser focus what will make your product a must-have-now! What are those few things that will make sense of all the other things? What is the senior or dominant buying motive in how your buyer will justify and validate this product as the right thing to purchase? The demonstration of your product is where you build value, create urgency, and increase the desire for your buyer to give you money for the product you are offering.

Cut the demonstration short and you only reduce your chances of making a sale. Spend too much time during the demonstration on things that the buyer doesn't find of value, and you not only waste time, but also reduce your chances at making a sale.

STEP FOUR: MAKE PROPOSAL

Make a proposal. I always make a proposal. Always. Even when people are not ready, I make an offer. Many people suggest not presenting all buyers with figures, but I believe that if you don't present them, you can never come to an agreement. I am not suggesting that you make an offer before the presentation of the product, but I am suggesting that you aggressively do what you can to get to figures with every buyer in every situation.

Always position yourself to present a proposal. Our goal is to present to 100 percent of those we greet, and to do so within forty minutes of contact. People need information to make a decision. We recently did a mystery shop of over five hundred similar companies and only 37 percent of them provided the mystery shopper with a proposal. That means that 63 percent never had a chance at the business beyond the shopper walking in. By shortening the sales process and insisting on getting to figures, we have taken companies and increased their sales 35 percent in a thirty-day period. We did this recently with a retail group in Boston, whereby we provided online training daily and drove their sales team toward one objective—presenting a proposal. This alone resulted in $350,000 in gross profits in one month. See www.CardoneUniversity.com.

STEP FIVE: CLOSE THE DEAL OR EXIT

This is where we find out how much game you have. You have to check out two things that I created: Close the Sale app and my *Closer's Survival Guide* book and audio program, which train salespeople to be masters at the close.

First, you must be prepared to CLOSE. Closing the transaction is a completely different art from selling. We were all born to sell, but you have to learn how to close. By survey, this is the one area in which professional salespeople demand help. This is where you must become a PRO-NINJA-MASTER CLOSER OF ALL SITUATIONS. A great closer needs hundreds of closes, not just a few. The pro needs a complete commitment to fresh and innovative ways to handle any closing situation that arises.

Stalls, money objections, price objections, budget considerations, better offers, and the like are only some of what you will hear from your clients. Becoming a pro at closing the transaction is critical not just because that is what it takes to get the job done, but also because it will create a confidence in your ability to handle objections, stalls, and problems, which will increase your confidence to do more selling. Salespeople who can't close will start to avoid all the other vital necessities of selling, such as prospecting, following up, and even having a positive attitude. Basically, why sell if you can't close? One hundred percent of your income results because of closed transactions. This is where you get paid. Approach this skill like you would if you were attempting to get a third-degree black belt. A couple of crazy closing programs are *My Closers Survival* book and audio, which I will be expanding from one volume to three. And my website www.CloseOrLose.com. These programs have hundreds of closing responses for EVERY objection you will ever hear in a negotiation.

CHAPTER NINETEEN
SUCCESS IN SELLING

*Treat success as your duty, obligation, and responsibility, not as a
choice or as a job!*

The best advice I can give you about success in any field is to
make being successful an ethical issue, not a financial issue or
even a technical issue. Almost all people claim they want success,
but most people approach it as only a possible option. Approach
anything as an option or a maybe, and I assure you that it will
NEVER be yours.

Did you know that less than 2 percent of all the households
in America made $250,000 last year? Why? Well either the whole
system is set up against 98 percent of the people, or 98 percent of
the people are treating success as something that may or may not
happen. Look, the reality is that the top earners are not smarter
than you, nor do they work harder. One of the major reasons

more people don't create success for themselves is because they never commit to it. They leave it to the economy, timing, and other happenstance that they have no control over.

Let's face it, most people don't even get close to creating the kind of life they want, and even fewer create the kind of life they have the potential to create. People claim they want a successful relationship, claim they want financial freedom, claim they want a successful, solvent business, claim they want more money, and claim they want to be millionaires, but then they don't go after these wants with a relentless, undying, gotta-have-it-now kind of pursuit.

ASK YOURSELF THESE QUESTIONS

- Are you fulfilling your potential? (Be honest.)
- Do you approach success as a duty and obligation?
- Would more success be bad for you?
- Is your entire family on one plan for the creation of success?

If you answered no to any of the above, your chances at success are doubtful in any field. Your problem will not be sales as a profession, it will be that you haven't made a commitment to SUCCESS as your obligation and duty. In sales, like any other field, you will have to demand success, otherwise it will elude you. Quit approaching success as an option, and your chances of reaching your dreams will rise exponentially. I can assure you that if you don't consider it your duty to live up to your potential, then you simply *won't* live up to your potential. If success doesn't become an ethical issue for you—an obsession and a must—then you won't do what is necessary to attain it. Many suggest that success is a journey rather than a destination. After building four businesses from scratch, I can tell you that while success may be a journey, it is more important to understand that the journey is filled with many unexpected obstacles, and lots of people are on the same journey. Other people and obstacles will attempt to stop you from reaching your destination. Those who make a commitment to success as a destination will last longer than those who are just on a journey.

One of the greatest turning points in my sales career occurred when I finally woke up to the fact that if I was going to be successful in sales, I had to make it a priority—a career, not a job. When I stopped thinking about selling casually and committed to knowing everything there was to know about it, I started to create success. When I started approaching selling as my way to create success and took it on as a duty, obligation, and responsibility, like a military mission, the obstacles that came with selling started to just fade away. I began to see that my sales success wasn't for others or "the lucky," or something that happened one week but not the next.

Even the most fortunate and well-connected people among us must do something to put themselves in the right places, at the right times, in front of the right people. Luck is just one of the by-products of those who take the most action and are the most prepared. The reason that successful salespeople seem lucky is because their success naturally allows for more success. Unless you are privy to the action, you don't see or hear about the number of times the top salespeople went for it and failed. Luck will not make you successful; committing yourself to success completely is the way to be lucky.

You have to approach your sales success the way good parents approach their duty to their children: As an honor, an obligation, and a priority. Be committed to your career, your product, the company you work for, and to your client as a duty, obligation, and responsibility. As in the chapter "The Most Important Sale," you have to stay completely committed at all levels. Good parents will do *whatever* it takes to care for children: Get up in the middle of the night; clothe, feed, and fight for them; take care of them; and even put their own lives at risk to protect them. This is the same way you must approach your sales career.

BE HONEST WITH YOURSELF: NEVER JUSTIFY FAILURE

It is fairly common for people who are not succeeding in sales to start justifying why they are not being successful. Some even start to lie to themselves. It's easy to spot this trend in the sales industry in the people who were once doing well and who are now making more and more excuses for why they are not succeeding. Read the "10X Rule" chapter about excuses where I go over all the excuses people use on themselves.

When young children, for example, are unable to get what they want, they ask nicely, then they get disappointed, then they start to insist on having what they want, and maybe even fight for a little while and cry for a bit. Then, toward the end of the cycle, when they have been told that they cannot have what they asked for, they start to convince themselves that they never wanted it in the first place. Sell or Be Sold. All children usually have to do is go through the cycle a few more times before the parent is worn down. When you aren't honest with yourself, you give up! There is NO reason or excuse good enough for you not to get what you want or need! Clearly you aren't always going to make the sale, but please don't fail to make one sale and then spend the rest of the afternoon selling yourself lies and excuses about why it wasn't important or why you weren't successful.

Be honest with yourself on every sales cycle. Ask yourself, "Why didn't I get that sale? What could I have done differently? Where did I miss it? How could I have better justified the cost? Where could I have gotten them financing? Why didn't I get in front of the decision maker? I only asked for the order twice . . ." Be honest, brutally honest, with yourself, and take complete responsibility for the outcome. Don't let your coworkers console you that it's all right, the customer wasn't ready, they didn't have the money, they are cheap, they are a difficult group to sell, they never buy, they can't make decisions, our product is too high, we don't have the right inventory, the economy sucks—please stop it. You are boring me and killing yourself by not being honest.

Your sales success will come about as the result of your mental, spiritual, and technically prepared claim to create and own it, followed by taking necessary actions that persist over time until you succeed in reaching your sales goals. If you are not able to be brutally honest with yourself about why you didn't make the sale, you will forever find your results dwindling. And when your success dwindles, you will see your actions start to do the same.

In order to demand consistent sales success, you have to:

1. Decide you are ultimately responsible for the sale.
2. Make it your duty, obligation, and responsibility to make the sale.
3. Take massive amounts of action, followed by more action until the sale is made!
4. Accept no excuses, reasons, or logic, and figure out how to make it work!
5. Prepare yourself daily to handle all obstacles, stalls, reasons, and barriers you will encounter with a client. See Cardone University at www.CardoneUniversity.com.

CHAPTER TWENTY

SALES-TRAINING TIPS

It is not enough to just read a book or listen to an audio program; you have to practice, drill, and rehearse. From astronauts to athletes they all practice, drill, and rehearse—over and over again until each move, response, and reaction has been worked out. A Navy Seal submerses himself in his training so that he not only knows exactly what to do in any situation, but also to give himself supreme confidence so that when a situation presents itself he can move aggressively into victory rather than having to back off.

If you find yourself backing off anywhere in the sales game, it is because you are not submersing yourself enough in training and education and then practicing-drilling-rehearsing. When I got serious about sales, I watched videos of sales instructions before I left my home, listened to audio programs on the drive to work, and then recorded myself in closing situations each day. I immersed myself in situations and handlings.

I would tell you to spend as much money and time on your training each month as you do on your wardrobe. Let me tell you, what you say and how you act will have more to do with a sale than what you wear. I could wear anything to work and sell my products when my game is tight. If you played professional baseball, would you go to the batting cage every day? Of course you would.

While it is agreed that training can improve production results, most people don't know the right way to train. And before you consider the cost, what you need to think about is the time you will set aside to train, because that is a bigger issue. If I get you on the right training schedule that truly builds sales muscle, training that results in increased sales, the money issue will be resolved. Did you know that most salespeople don't even read one sales book in their entire career? Did you also know that even fewer people spend any quality time practicing selling? And even those who do don't know how to train effectively to get results immediately. What I am talking about here is giving you a training regimen that will turn you into a super salesperson.

Before you consider the cost of sales-training books, seminars, videos, audio programs, workshops, and travel and lodging, you should calculate the immediate costs of mishandling opportunities that result from not training. Regardless of how long you have been in sales, if you are rusty, you are rusty. A dull saw might cut the tree down, but it will take much longer than is necessary. To keep the sales saw sharp, you have to spend time sharpening it. Sales training has failed companies and individuals because it has been incorrectly implemented, not measurable, outdated, not relevant, and wasn't readily available to solve sales problems when salespeople needed it the most.

After working with individuals and companies for more than twenty-five years, I have found that for any training program to be effective, there are certain criteria that must be adhered to:

1. Train daily! The material salespeople should read, listen to, or watch should be focused on selling situations, not just motivational ones.

2. Sales training should be approached with the goal to increase production immediately. Think about how Derek Jeter would use a batting cage prior to game time. Sales training is done daily in order to sharpen your skills for that day and make more sales! Training needs to be approached as a valuable and vital ingredient to increased production, and THE WAY to increased sales and revenue.

3. Sales training must be delivered in very short segments and should be interactive. What is short? Two to five minutes and shorter. Most training fails today just because the segments are too long and they lose the attention of the trainee. Our on-demand interactive training sites utilize multimedia interactive engagement in order to provide sales professionals with very concise, short segments that are focused on exact sales situations.

4. Training must be measurable and rewarded. Training that is not easily measurable, like any process or best practice, will fail. If it doesn't increase production immediately, then it is either not being used or not being used enough. The correct way to set this up is to provide you with daily reminders when training is not being used.

5. Effective sales-training programs should focus 80 percent of the training content, time, and energy on the TOP people in an organization, not the new ones. If the content is truly relevant and cutting edge, rather than just a repeat of the basics over and over again, it should get the attention of top performers.

6. Sales training should be made part of your day and should be accessible continually throughout the day. All staff meetings should include training, with salespeople following that up with a minimum of two to four segments each day on their own, and then the sales team should be supported with sales solutions during the day. We added this last component via our virtual technology whereby salespeople can interactively consult me in real time, and I am actually able to coach them through a transaction and demonstrate ways to close more deals. This combination of training throughout the day is similar to how you would correctly hydrate the body with the fluids in an IV drip.

For sales training to be effective, you need a commitment to it; it must be made the first thing each day, be a continued activity daily, be available when you need it, and increase your sales production. If you think it is expensive to train sales teams, think about the expense of missing sales.

MY TRAINING REGIMEN FOR YOU

- Daily: Listen to sales-training programs while driving. Cover topics such as handling objections, generating ideas for calling clients, following up, closing tips, and the like. Avoid hype and motivational material and focus on SALES-oriented strategies specifically.
- Daily: Watch two to four video segments that cover some part of the sales process.
- Role-play situations that you experience trouble with or find yourself withdrawing from.
- Use me as your personal coach during the day with our Quick Fix Solutions. Due to technological advances, I can assist you in real-time to make more sales. Check out www. CardoneUniversity.com. This is vital because after losing a sale, it is quite typical for you to make up wrong reasons for missing the sale and then get stuck with a wrong solution. With Quick Fix, you can prepare for a sale, get assistance during the sale, and also correct yourself after each encounter.

CHAPTER TWENTY-ONE

CREATE A SOCIAL MEDIA PRESENCE

With increasing numbers of people heading online as their first step to research your company, product, and even your personal information, it is mandatory that you create some type of social media presence. This is not a choice or something you either want to do or don't want to do, nor is it something you have or don't have time for: YOU MUST USE SOCIAL MEDIA.

Social media is a way for you to connect, prospect, and make yourself known to those who may have an interest in what you represent. As I wrote in *If You're Not First, You're Last*, obscurity (not being known) is a bigger problem than money. If people don't know who you are, then they cannot do business with you. If they know you but aren't thinking about you, they won't do business with you. You have to be known, thought about, considered, and hopefully, the first or dominating choice in your clients' minds in order to ever sell anything to anyone!

Today it is Facebook, Twitter, LinkedIn, Google+, and who knows what will come next. One day I am sure these names won't even exist, having been replaced by some other technological improvements. These names today are like the newspaper ads of early newspapers or the first billboards that showed up alongside highways and city streets years ago. Social media, except for the time it takes, is a free way for you to make yourself known. The key is you have to know HOW to use it rather than be used by it. Social media for the most part is like walking into a bar or party. You may mention business at the party or to the person in the bar, but you are probably more likely to talk about more social things than straight business. If you want a good example of how to use social media, check out the following pages that I created to demonstrate to people how to get interaction and involvement: Twitter@grantcardone and www.facebook.com/cardonesuccess. Watch how much interaction, feedback, and involvement I get while still pushing who I am.

The other thing that forces you to take a position with social media is your public and/or company reputation. Ten years ago, if someone wasn't satisfied with the service at the resort they stayed at in some tropical paradise, they simply told a handful of friends and relatives. Today they are more likely to post a review online, and thousands of people, related and unrelated, may see it. The worst part is that the posted comment may not even be a fair assessment of the resort's overall service.

It only takes a few bad reviews or complaints about you, your company, or your product to result in lost opportunities and a damaged perception of you and your brand. Your customers are online, and it is critical to manage your online reputation in order to protect your brand, as it may be the first impression the public gets about you.

Social tools like Yelp, Facebook, Twitter, YouTube, and thousands of blogging sites with endless agendas have magnified the voices of your clients and potential prospects for your business. Let's face it: Almost anything can get posted about you or your company regardless of the facts. Also, it is more likely that a disgruntled person is going to take the time to post than a happy one because the disgruntled person has so much attention tied up in what he perceived as a negative experience or exchange.

No matter who you are or what your business is, when you start getting attention and creating any success at all, it is only a matter of time before someone will post something negative about you online. This is an impossible avoidance. The only way not to get attention is to hide under a rock, and even then you will be discovered. With the influence of social media, those who are critical of you, maybe even those who are envious you, and those who compete with your product or your company can easily show up online to bash you.

Criticism, dissatisfied customers, varying opinions, opposition, and even intentional and malicious brand-bashing are not new challenges in business. These issues have been around since the creation of gossip and competition; it is the power, accessibility, and reach of the Web that makes your social media reputation a new issue.

Here are some ideas about how you can manage negative social media:

1. Treat your social media reputation like your personal reputation. Handle social media attacks the same way you would a personal attack. Handle such attacks, don't delegate this or take it lightly. Nothing is more important than your name and reputation.

2. Handle ALL negative posts as opportunities. All complaints, bashing, and customer dissatisfactions should be treated as opportunities, not problems (until proven to be something else). A dissatisfied customer or negative post can be turned into a fan or compliment when handled correctly. I have a policy in my company in which I personally contact every customer who expresses a complaint. My goal is to transform any problem into a win for everyone.

3. Handle immediately. The sooner you handle the complaint, the easier it handles. Respond immediately and reasonable people will appreciate you making them a priority. Don't respond with the intent for them to remove a post or criticism, but rather respond by addressing their concern. "Wow, I saw what you posted online and I wanted to call you right away and see what I could do to handle it. I had no idea. Tell me about what happened. What can I do to resolve it?" Most people, when handled correctly, will then retract the post or post how great you are.

4. Contact directly. Do not respond publicly online to something negative, as you only bring more attention to it. Like any communication, it is best when handled directly either by phone, a direct message, or even in person if possible. Be careful not to suggest wrongdoing in your message, but

instead let the party know you want to see what you can do to handle the upset.

5. Be proactive. The best solution to reputation management is to be on offense not defense. Create initiatives to collect positive posts and testimonials, even videos, about you and your company. Encourage and make it easy for the people who love and do business with you to spread the good word about you. Aggressively build a positive public relations campaign about your good works, endeavors, and contributions that will outweigh any negative post. Call us if you want some direction about how you can establish a strong social media reputation.

6. Know your limitations. While I believe that every complaint is an opportunity, you have to know which battles to fight and which ones to walk away from. There are some people whose real goals are to consume you, your focus, and your energy. They don't seek resolution; they seek to consume you like a vampire. There are some people who are only interested in making noise, negativity, and spewing hate. Disregard and don't engage them once they prove they are only interested in the negative.

The most important thing is you should treat your social media reputation in the same manner you would your personal and public reputation. It is only a matter of time before someone posts negative comments about you, which may include exaggerations of dissatisfaction issues, with some going as far as fabricating complete falsehoods. It is a fact of life that to the degree you get attention, you will at some point get criticism.

Protecting your online reputation requires that you know what you can do so that the public searching you out gets the right story about you. Make it a priority and be proactive!

Lastly, the number one excuse for not using social media is not having the time. And, I agree, you don't have time to waste on social media like 99 percent of users do, but you must learn to use social media as a way to save time. Make time, make yourself known, and establish a strong social media reputation. I personally work three Facebook pages, one Twitter feed, and one Google+ account. It isn't a waste of time that will keep you from doing this; it is only a lack of commitment and understanding of what it can do for you.

$250,000 SALE SUCCESS SCHEDULE

$250,000 Prosperity Schedule
"Go to Work to Prosper, Not to Work."

6 am	Wake up (rule is two hours before you need to be somewhere)
	Write long-term goals
	Exercise and listen/watch motivational training (control your input)
7 am	Dress for success
	Make driving time learning time (should be sales-training content)
	Eat out: Be seen among prospective clients
7:45 am	Arrive early to office
	Create battle plan for short-term targets
	Daily sales meeting (short, positive, twenty minutes max)

Create hot list of who you can get in front of today

Save-a-deal meeting: Past deals list with save plan

Massive outbound action using battle plan

Follow up 100 percent of yesterday's opportunities (no exceptions)

Call five clients regarding service updates

Call last week mailers/e-mails out

Fax blast all of last week's opportunities

Noon   Call client list for lunch

Either lunch out with client or be seen out where they are

1–5 pm   Massive outflow

Send mailers to five sold customers

Send mailers to all traffic ten days old

Send out five mailers to friends

Send out five mailers to business contacts

Send out five birthday cards

Personal visits to clients at office before day over

5–8 pm   Handle appointments and walk-in traffic

Continue to work the phone til day end

8–10 pm   Update tomorrow's battle plan

Go home/be 100 percent with loved ones

Avoid TV

Make a list of great contacts to make the rest of the week

Write your long-terms goals again

Try to sleep

THE PROFESSIONAL SALESPERSON'S DAILY COMMITMENTS

I commit to working my plan every day!

I commit to a "can do" attitude with every customer!

I commit to doing whatever it takes!

I commit to exceeding the expectations of my customers!

I commit to staying focused on what I want!

I commit to taking every opportunity all the way!

I commit to following up on every opportunity!

I commit to being highly ethical in every area of my life!

I commit to making changes where necessary!

I commit to educating myself every day!

I commit to training every day!

I commit to doing the right thing!

I commit to being the most positive person I know!

I commit to quit making excuses and just make it happen!

I commit to making my dreams come true by my actions!

THE TEN COMMANDMENTS OF SALES

Commandment #1: Be Proud and Be Positive

Dress like you are proud, act like you are proud, and be the most positive person your customer will ever meet.

Commandment #2: Dress for Sales Success

Commandment #3: See the Sale

Customers don't make sales, the salesperson does. If you leave it up to the customer, nothing will happen. If you can't see it happening it never will. You must see the sale before it actually takes place. You have to know that you can get the sale done and see the customer owning your product and going to the register or into ownership with you. If you don't see it, it will not happen.

Commandment #4: Be Sold on Your Offer

This is the most important of all sales. If you can't make this sale, you won't make many of the ones that pay you! I know salespeople who sell products they don't even own. How can you do this and expect to sell your products? Each week I write a list of the reasons people should own my products and why they are worth the investment.

Commandment #5: Know Your Value Proposition

Your value proposition most often has nothing to do with your product. What do you bring to the table that sets your proposal apart from all others? Find out what is of value to them—what would you have to see that would cause you to take action?

Commandment #6: Always Agree with Your Client

When you hear something you object to or disagree with, handle it with agreement, not disagreement. Even if the customer is wrong about something, there is no value by telling him so. Always, always, always agree with your client: "You are right," "I agree," "I am with you!" It is often better to just acknowledge your client than to try to handle the client. Sometimes, "I agree with you" is enough.

Commandment #7: Super Freak Demonstration

Make sure you demonstrate double the value in your demonstration of a product. No one spends $200,000 on something that is worth $200,000. They only spend $200,000 when they believe they are getting something of value in excess of what they are spending. Super freak your presentation so that people can't live without your offer.

Commandment #8: Be Time Efficient

The buyer of the twenty-first century is in a hurry. My goal is to do as much selling as I can in the shortest period of time possible. Shortcutting will only cost you more time. Spending more time with your client will NOT ensure a sale, but in fact will negatively affect your closing ratio and gross profits. Spending quality time and knowing what your buyer values will save all parties time.

Commandment #9: Assume the Close

"Follow me and I will show you how easy it is to own your new _____." "If there aren't any other reasons for taking the next logical step, follow me." Make it difficult to say no by not asking a question and just moving forward. "Follow me" and "sign here" are two of the most powerful phrases to a salesperson.

Commandment #10: Always Persist in the Close

Until a transaction is closed, you have provided no value to your client. Most salespeople never attempt to close one time, much less persist enough times to get the sale. "Sign here" are the words of a closer; being able to handle all the stalls and objections that surface is what determines whether you will be successful or not!

CHAPTER TWENTY-TWO

QUICK TIPS TO CONQUER THE BIGGEST CHALLENGES IN SELLING

Salespeople were surveyed to discover what their biggest challenges were in selling. Their top answers have been compiled in this chapter. Whether one of these is an issue for you or not, or ever becomes one, you might be interested in what others suggest their challenges are and my brief thoughts on each one.

REJECTION

Rejection is not a sales issue. It is part of the human condition and an experience or illusion created by the person experiencing it. If you don't like rejection, well that makes you more normal than abnormal. I have never met anyone who does. Also, if you think you can avoid rejection, sorry, you are on the wrong planet.

If there is something you want and you ask someone to help you with it, and that person declines, then you experience rejection. So you either walk away disappointed, rejected, and sad, or you dig in and figure out how to get that person to support what it is you want.

For example, is a homeless person rejected when he gets told no when he asks for a quarter? Maybe. Or maybe he needs to change his presentation and offer. A rich boy asks a girl out and the girl says no. Was he rejected? Maybe he needs to change his presentation and offer and not come off like the rich guy who always gets what he wants. See, in this case I took two extremes and both were told no.

I think the experience of rejection as an emotion is actually what happens when a person has a low responsibility level in getting things done. "I didn't get what I want, so now I am going to feel sorry for myself, label it rejection, and act like a victim." Ain't nothing happening to you; it's happening 'cause of you!

How you handle rejection is the key. Try to avoid it and you are doomed because you will withdraw. If you start to think less of your product or offer after being told no, then you are being sold on someone else's agenda. When you are told "no," or "not yet," or "we bought from someone else," have you been rejected? You will only feel rejection as a negative sensation if you do not take full responsibility for the situation.

When I am told no I don't equate it with rejection; I look at what I could do differently next time to earn their business. How could I be more effective? How could I turn this person into a customer next time? No one says to you, "I am rejecting you," they merely say no to the offer. You are creating an illusion that it is rejection. Rejection is experienced by those unwilling to be responsible for the outcome.

NEGATIVE SURROUNDINGS

This is a major complaint from salespeople: Being surrounded by environments that are negative. The ease at which people can get into sales and then the unfortunate low demands put on sales organizations to learn the craft can create negative environments.

But all you have to do is sit in front of a TV and see that most of this planet is negative. The problem with negativity anywhere is that it is a disease and is contagious by nature, affecting everyone in its vicinity. When you put negative people into a sales environment, it is destructive to your ability to be focused, productive, and effective. The last thing a client wants is negativity. People can get that without a sales presentation. It is my belief that your clients will pay more for a positive attitude than they will for a great product.

It will be critical to your sales success that you keep your environment positive. That includes your physical environment as well as what goes on between your ears. Trust me, you will hear enough negativity from the media and clients. The last thing you need is people you work around or your family adding to it.

Make it known that you will not tolerate negative thinking or talk around you. Post it up in your office that it is not tolerated any more than you would allow someone to leave trash or filth in your space. Take a hard stance with everyone close to you: NO NEGATIVITY ALLOWED HERE. If you don't have something positive to say, then go away until you do! Negative talk or references about clients should be against the rules and reprimanded by management. Negative talk about your product line, the company, or management should immediately indicate the person is operating as an enemy of the group. If people can't bring solutions and improvements and all they offer is negativity, then they are enemies to you, the company, and even themselves.

DISCIPLINE

Probably the single most important factor to any success is the ability to show up day after day and do the right things. The person, company, or team that is unable to deliver disciplined actions is going to experience ups and downs.

In sales, lacking discipline is going to negatively impact your presentation, motivation, ability to predict results, follow-up, and your ability to keep your pipeline full. Lack of discipline is rampant in sales because so many sales positions are commission based. This allows the salesperson to believe he or she can self-manage and get away with spotty undisciplined activity. The economy will discipline anyone who operates with this sense of freedom. If you want sales success, you must exercise discipline. That is why I provided you with a schedule.

White space on a calendar is a disaster for the salesperson. Keep your schedule full, stay busy, and always be moving forward. Discipline the little things like when you go to sleep, when you wake up, the first thing you do each day, when you get to work, how you start each day, etc. The reason discipline is so important in sales is because there are so many random things happening, so the more stability you can personally create, the more secure you will be and the more certain your results.

THE ECONOMY

The economy is a source of concern for all sales organizations and salespeople. When times are good and people and companies are spending money, it would appear easier to sell. But in good times the competition is even more fierce. When the economy gets very tight, uncertain, and is more contracted, selling becomes more difficult because people are more careful with their expenditures.

I personally achieve more when economies are contracting than when they are expanding because it is a time for me to use my other skills, such as work ethic, discipline, and a positive attitude, to stand apart. When people are so focused on how "bad" the economy is, I am able to get accounts I might not have been able to get before. People make many mistakes during contracting economies because they incorrectly respond to contraction.

Tough economies result in contracted spending and investments, uncertainty in making decisions, tighter lending by banks, and more. This is when the professional and his skills will win the game. If you are in sales long enough, you will experience stagnant economies, great economies, and terrible economies. Be prepared for all of them. In selling, you can create your own economy rather than being a participant in what everyone else has agreed upon as the economy. Take advantage of all types of economies, because you will experience them all and they all offer opportunities.

COMPETITION

In my seminars, I am always going to have someone ask me, "What do I do about the guy who sells an inferior/similar/same product for less than I am?" My question is, "What about the competitor who has a superior product and sells for less than you!?"

My answer to the situation is, "What are you doing competing?" Don't compete; dominate with your product, company, personality, and your offer. If you aren't the difference maker, then others will forever outsell you with a cheaper price or better offer. No product stays superior forever! Sooner or later, someone is going to create a better X, and then you are going to experience lower prices and fewer sales followed by less success.

In my book, *The 10X Rule*, I talk about competition being for sissies. You don't want to compete; you want to dominate a sector. The goal is to provide your client with so much attention, follow-up, and service that you can't be competed with. Find a way to differentiate yourself. The value proposition should always be what you bring to the table.

A client once told me, "I can get a better deal from so-and-so." And I said, "I don't come with that transaction. Sign here, and let's get on with it." And he signed. Don't compete; own and dominate your sector!

PRODUCT KNOWLEDGE

Products are changing so fast today it is almost impossible to keep up. Whether it is the menu in the restaurant, the 38,718 products in the grocery store, regulations on mortgages and financial products, or the technical advances of all mass-manufactured goods, product knowledge is a very big challenge to salespeople.

Regardless of the industry you are in or the product you sell, there will be advances that make your product current and appealing to your client. With that comes the challenge of staying in the know on those improvements. The only salespeople this is a problem for are those who are not committed, those who don't make time to study up, and those who overestimate product knowledge as a sales solution.

If you aren't committed, you are going to get crushed, and product knowledge will only be one of your excuses. If you don't take the time to study up, you are going to lose credibility with your clients and it will be painful. And, lastly, if you overestimate product knowledge as a solution, you will be gravely disappointed.

With the advent and ease of the Internet, 90 percent of all buyers are going online to check out their next purchase or investment. With that comes both misinformation and accurate information. But the good news is that they are still requesting some information from the salesperson to assist them in making their decision. Don't get bogged down in product knowledge, but do learn enough about the product to stay credible and also to customize your value ad proposition. Remember, very few buyers want a drill for the sake of a drill; most of them want it for the hole it will make, and even more want it because of the problem it will solve!

FOLLOW-UP

This has to be the greatest weakness of salespeople and sales organizations. More often than not, when I have an experience with a company or individual, I am not followed up. And when I am followed up, it is only once or twice, and then I am forgotten or written off as a waste of time.

Even my company errs here with not following up enough with clients. There are thousands of customer relationship management (CRM) tools that have been created with the hope of solving this problem. Some companies even hire telemarketers to ensure the follow-up.

The best salespeople I know are those who are great at following up, staying connected, staying in touch, and using creativity to keep their sold and unsold clients thinking about them. Following up someone who you just sold is one thing and offers its own challenges. Then there is following up the unsold who has not bought yet. Add to that the person who was unsold and bought from someone else. What about the person, company, or account manager who you know will buy your product in the future but has yet to show an interest?

All of these are follow-up opportunities that offer different challenges and require different creativity. Follow-up requires an undying clarity about your purpose and staying sold on yourself to get it all. I am not interested in *some* of the market; I want to get *all* of it. Great follow-up requires commitment, perpetual motivation, a can-do attitude, a never quit mentality, organizational skills, support, reminders, and lots of creativity, fortitude, and persistence.

There are clients whom I have followed up for ten years before I ever earned their business. There are clients I have now as I write this that pop into my mind whose business I have yet to earn: A book publisher, a publicly held automotive company with more than 3,400 locations, an international production company that

I want to get in front of, and more. With follow-up, you don't know when they are going to finally come around.

Staying committed and creative is key, and even more important is you staying interested and not forgetting about your clients. When you forget about them, they are certain to forget about you. Remember what I did with the greatest sale of my life—winning the date with my wife—I stayed interested, continued to find creative ways to get in front of her, and now she is stuck with me for this lifetime.

ORGANIZATION

Keeping organized is a challenge for me because I move at two hundred miles per hour and create lots of activity and unfinished cycles around me. This means I need either organization or someone else picking up the pieces and organizing the past actions and next actions to take. Moving fast doesn't mean I wouldn't like to be organized.

I like order, as it gives me a sense of control, and I love control! Good organization skills allow you to put more in a piece of luggage and find it, or even better, to travel light, only bringing that which was needed. Organization allows me to find things faster, make contact quicker, and hopefully get more done. The type of organization that just slows things down is a different type of organization than we are talking about here.

Organization is critical in order to be able to later find things, follow up, and identify what you know about a client and where to pick up with that client. There are what seem like endless CRMs, filing, storing, and follow-up tools available today to organize you better. The issue is figuring out how to use these tools, as they are

only going to put things in place for you; you will still need to dig
them out.

Organization is critical to the salesperson, so take some time
to make sure you record EVERY potential client interaction with
cell numbers, e-mail addresses, photos, assistants' names, hot buttons, likes and dislikes, family, and what is vital to the individual.
Regardless of the outcome of your interaction, do not EVER dis-
card data. Even when you leave your current scene, make sure you
maintain those contacts because you might find you need them
in the future.

Your ability to organize your space, your thinking, your clients, your office, and your own physical environment are important to organizing your success.

CALL RELUCTANCE

This is the phenomenon whereby an individual creates reasons
not to actively and aggressively call on clients. Salespeople have
suffered from this issue for years.

Anytime you aren't calling on a client, you are participating
in some form of call reluctance. Paperwork, organizing your desk,
filing, calculating possible commissions, counting money, gossiping, and hanging out at the watercooler are just a few examples
of call reluctance. This costs salespeople more than anything they
will ever spend money on.

Call reluctance ultimately comes from not being constantly
motivated and trained at your job as a salesperson. When you
KNOW what to do, what to say, how to handle objections, get
appointments, and handle stalls and other challenges, you will

not experience call reluctance. The length of time someone has been doing sales does not protect him or her from call reluctance.

Salespeople who are motivated, regularly trained, and, especially, those involved in train-drill-rehearse exercises are less apt to fall victim to call reluctance. Call reluctance is not a disease and does not mean you are not cut out for sales. Call reluctance is an indication of a lack of training, motivation, and education that builds confidence in the sales professional.

FILL THE PIPELINE

Sales is a numbers game to some degree. If you have a 100 percent closing ratio and only call on one person in your career, then you can only be so successful. Keeping the pipeline full at all times is vital to success.

Most salespeople only measure who they recently sold, but you should value and measure all activities that fill the pipeline: Sold, unsold, lost to competitor, orders, not ready to buy until next quarter, referrals, second sales, etc. One of the common mistakes I see from salespeople and sales organizations is that they celebrate sales and don't keep loading up the pipeline. One of the negatives of selling a client is that you lose the client and then have to start the cycle again with someone else. This is what I mean about keeping the pipeline full.

It takes a lot of work to sell someone and immediately replace him or her with someone else. I talk a lot in my book *The 10X Rule* about the fact that people underestimate the amount of energy and effort necessary to create success, and then to maintain that success. Conquering something is one thing; keeping it is another thing entirely. In sales, you want a full pipeline of possibilities so you aren't dependent on the success of any one thing. Salespeople without full pipelines become desperate and easily shaken. A guy who works with me called and was complaining about a prospect who canceled an appointment, and I told him, "If your pipeline was full, you would be happy he canceled, not upset. You are upset not because he canceled, but because you failed to fill up your pipeline!"

Fill up your pipeline, keep it full, overrun it if you choose, and never think you have enough in it.

CLOSING THE DEAL

Negotiating and closing the transaction can be a trouble spot for salespeople. I believe this to be the case mostly because closing is not selling. Closing has been taught as though it is a sales technique, but it is only an extension of selling and is, in actuality, a completely different art.

Selling is identifying needs, selecting the right solution, and then demonstrating how your product or service solves the problem. Closing is getting the buyer to take action and agree to exchange something of value for what it is you offer; that is, close on your offer and solution.

I have met professional salespeople who were good at building rapport and getting people to like them, good at getting people excited about their product/service, and good at follow-up, and while all those skills are important, if they couldn't close they weren't successful.

Great salespeople know that all it takes to be great at selling is to take the time to become pros at negotiating and closing so they can take advantage of the investments made in the selling process prior to closing the transaction. Just because someone can wrestle doesn't mean they can box or fight in the UFC. Closing is an art, and anyone can learn it. Closing requires a tremendous arsenal of techniques, transitions, responses, counters, and strategies.

The single most productive decision I made in selling was my commitment to master the close. I have created numerous tools that people can use to make themselves masters at this thing called closing. Check out our app at www.CloseTheSaleApp.com. Also check into my *Closer's Survival Guide: Volume I*, which includes 126 closes. This work is being followed up with two more volumes. Another effective closing education tool, if you like to learn visually, is my virtual training site, which delivers more than 300 closes in full-motion videos on demand.

CALLS NOT RETURNED

In my career, more people have not returned my call than have taken my call. You need to understand that when people do not call you back, it does not mean they are not interested in you or your product. It could mean that, but it doesn't have to mean that. Maybe they didn't get your message, perhaps they got overwhelmed with other things, or maybe they just don't feel a sense of manners that requires them to return phone calls.

I personally make an effort to respond to all calls made to me regardless of my interest in the call or caller. And if I can't get to the call, then I will have my assistant respond, requesting either more information or informing the person that I am not interested. I just think it's important for me to keep the flow of communication open from others to me and then from me to others. If I stop communicating either way, I think I might stop other flows that are necessary.

Now, just because I take people's calls and respond to calls and e-mails doesn't mean other people do or should. I never take it personally when people don't call me back. I always, always, always leave a message when I call someone. And then I keep calling them back regardless of whether I get a response from them or not. When someone doesn't call you back, don't try to calculate what their lack of response means.

CALL CLIENT + LEFT MESSAGE + NO RETURN CALL = ?????????

You don't know what it means when a client does not call you back, but what it should mean is that you need to continue to make calls, contacts, e-mails, or personal visits until you find out what it means! Just because the client is not interested in you today doesn't mean he will not be interested in you tomorrow. Just because you are not a priority this week or this afternoon doesn't mean you should quit calling.

Never bring up unreturned previous calls and never make the client wrong for not calling you back. It's not his or her job, responsibility, or agreement to call you back. It is your job to do the follow-up, and the more creative and persistent you can be the better. Vary the types of communications and vary the messages—keep it creative. If e-mails aren't working, try postage. If that doesn't work, try calls and then personal visits. If none of that works, I always put clients on a "help-list" and then ask other clients if they can help me with anyone on the list. Sometimes it's just a matter of getting the right person at the right time. Remember, quitting can't be an option, and making the client wrong is just you not taking responsibility. Nothing is happening *to* you; it is happening because of you.

FEAR

The great thing about fear is that it isn't real. I know that when you are experiencing fear it might feel real, but it actually does not exist in the physical universe. This unseen, intangible factor called fear does so much to motivate some, yet it also immobilizes millions of people every day from taking the actions they need to take. Pretty powerful stuff, right? With sales, fear can kill your chances of success, but here's the secret: The way to kill fear is by taking action. There's nothing like an unshakable, winning flurry of action to absolutely extinguish that monster called fear (that, and a great sense of humor).

I use fear every day as my inspiration—as an indicator of those things I have to confront. Catch my phrasing: "I *use* fear." It's not the other way around. Fear, although not a real thing, is very powerful, and I'm big enough to admit to feeling it. My success is that I then use it to move—in fact, to move toward exactly that thing of which I am the most afraid. This is an existential exercise you can do by first asking yourself, "Can I face my fears?" The more you practice moving in the direction of that which you fear, the more it becomes a habit, second nature in fact. You could even start your day by asking, "Who or what do I most fear calling on today?" The answer should give you direction in which to move. Taking action on those things you fear is how you build courage.

Courage is an exercise in action, it's not just a trait. Everyone has the ability to be courageous; you just have to take action. Do this and you will get to the point where you start looking around for more things that you fear. Because, hey, doing them is actually a lot of fun and there is a payoff in both confidence and success.

When I turned forty-five, my wife, who was my fiancé at the time, thought she would surprise me by taking me skydiving for the first time. She had jumped three times and was going to try to scare me by giving me a surprise jump for my birthday. I didn't know the first thing about jumping, and she wanted to see me get scared. Was I scared? Yeah, of course, but I kept telling myself, "Getting overwhelmed won't open your chute." The hardest part was the ascent 10,000 feet into the air, anticipating the jump to my possible death. The list of all the things that could go wrong filled my mind during that twenty-minute ride up, but I kept telling myself, "The more you do that which you fear, the more courageous you become. Being scared won't open the chute."

I looked over and saw my beautiful, confident fiancé by my side, looking at me, waiting for me to show fear, but I refused to do so. I gave her a look that I thought suggested, "I am scared of nothing," even though I was. She reached over to see if my heart was pounding, hoping to get a reaction. Not until they opened the door of the plane and people started jumping did it really hit me. Elena looked at me as she approached the opening, "See you on the ground, Sexy," she said, and she jumped out before me. That was when I really got scared because there was nothing I could do for her.

As I watched her fly through the sky, I really got it: I was about to jump. Rather than trying to process this, I elected to eat the fear and take action. I refused to be paralyzed by fear. I refused to be the slave of fear. I refused to let fear master me. Instead, I used fear to take action, and I rolled out of the plane. It was the decision to use fear that allowed me to take action. Not to mention the fact that my girl jumped; what was I going to do, puss out? When you do what you fear, you experience such gratification. As I fell through the sky, I was freed from any ideas of being held back by the boogeyman. Later, when I married that beautiful woman, I promised her I would always keep moving through those things I feared the most in order to provide us with a great future together.

Fear in your sales career and in life should be an indicator and motivator of what you need to do and must do! Overcoming your fear is just an exercise in doing something that will allow you to increase confidence in yourself and take your career to another level. Handling fear is merely a decision. So start building up this habit of identifying what you fear doing and who you fear calling on, and make those your first actions. I assure you that you will quickly build the confidence that is so critical for a sales professional to have. Like consistently working out in a gym, you will suddenly find your "fear-busting" muscle is really powerful, and taking actions in spite of your fear will no longer immobilize you. Instead, it will motivate you.

PEOPLE'S EMOTIONS

When you are faced with a prospect or client who gets emotional and demonstrates an emotional outburst with you, know that you are getting close to making the sale. Never take it personally, never react to it, and never become emotional, as a response. You must know that when people get highly emotional, typically they are getting close to completing the transaction. The key is to stay rational, calm, and collected when others get emotional, and persist no matter what is thrown your way. Emotions are one of the most overrated things there are. A guy gets angry because your proposal is double his budget. "I TOLD YOU I COULD ONLY AFFORD . . . !" Is he upset with you or himself? If double the budget is the best solution, then don't react to his outburst, just rationally handle it: "John, I am aware that this is double your budget. Allow me to share with you why I am showing you this option despite the fact that you made it clear to me you could only spend . . ." Stay calm. Stay cool. Stay rational, and know that the outburst will pass once your client comes to his senses.

Every person wants to make the best decision possible, so when you get him to face up to making a decision to buy your product, know that you are stirring up within him all the fears, failures, and frustrations of the past. You might be hitting up against his own sense of dissatisfaction with that idea that he can't easily afford this. Just because he shares his outburst with you and even directs it at you doesn't mean he is actually upset with you. Outbursts are usually not at all personal; they're just something that every person goes through. Some people just express themselves a bit more vocally than others, and they may go through a range of emotions in the process.

You cannot stop your pursuit of closing the sale every time someone gets upset. You must consistently and persistently help them because you are like their expert guide along a tumultuous river. You would of course not stop guiding them through the most dramatic rapids just because you hit white water and everyone started to freak. You would keep everyone calm, knowing that the white water doesn't last forever and soon you will be on the other side, where things are calm. Likewise, you want to guide your prospect through the sales process, through the dramatic, tough, emotional waters into the calm, happy state of him getting to have your product.

It is your duty to help your prospects in this way! Don't get emotional when they do. Practice, drill, and rehearse staying calm when others start freaking. This is a skill that can be developed but does take some drilling. The biggest problem for most people is when they experience someone getting highly emotional today, they are thrown back into some unresolved issue of the past when others were emotional with them, and it might have turned out badly. It is important that you are able to stay in the present when this happens; otherwise, you aren't going to be operating rationally, and if you aren't rational, you won't come up with solutions. Emotions are overrated, and the past is useless to you when creating a future. Stay calm, be cool, and learn how to stay rational when prospects get emotional.

NEGATIVE CONNOTATIONS OF SALES

The only reason that the subject of sales or salespeople has ever carried a negative connotation is because of inept salespeople who never took the time to become true professionals and master their craft. This lack of self-esteem about the career of sales comes from a lack of understanding about how vital salespeople are to economies and how different a SALES PRO is from a salesperson.

A true professional salesperson is impervious to any negativity because he is a pro and is operating at levels far beyond the average player of the game. That professional knows that to sell is to serve, and he or she believes so strongly in his product, service, company, and him- or herself that the motives that drive that individual are not just about "getting the commission." A true professional salesperson is motivated by truly helping others. A true professional salesperson is actually admired by all who he or she comes in contact with and is often celebrated by customers and colleagues alike.

If you feel yourself stymied by the negative connotation of being in sales, you simply need to reconnect to the purpose of what you're doing and the importance of selling as a career and to the development of entire economies. Reread the introduction and Chapter One of this book to enlighten your sense of purpose! I personally feel that selling is one of the noblest of professions because when done correctly and with the right intentions, it engenders a very independent, self-reliant, strong, helpful, and extroverted individual who is, indeed, at a higher level than most. A true professional salesperson is able to step into any circumstance and make friends, help others, calm the chaos, and get people to take action. Great salespeople are leaders and people who make sense of situations and inspire others to do the right thing!

Think of a person who has really helped you in your life, really positively affected you and made you feel good about yourself. Write down the five qualities that person had that made you feel good. Now write about how each of those qualities would make you a better salesperson.

In my life I have met some unbelievably exceptional

salespeople, and I never cease to be enamored by them. Their persistence, positive attitudes, listening skills, genuine interest, willingness to accept responsibility, desire to learn, and so many other attractive attributes are inspirational to me. Gavin, for instance, whom I mentioned previously, is a real pro and an exceptional master of his trade. He is always professionally dressed, and always positive, patient, persistent, understanding, and empathetic. He is a great listener, duplicates communication extremely well without buying into it completely, acknowledges me even when I am not making any sense, knows how to use humor, and is tremendously determined and focused on his mission of getting his deal done. These qualities make any individual attractive and separate Gavin from any negative connotations associated with salespeople. Because of these differences, he can pressure me without the "pressure" leaving a negative experience.

Become a pro in sales and people will have not disdain for you, but respect and admiration. No one dislikes a professional; it is the amateur who is resented in every field.

NOT HAVING THE RIGHT RESPONSE

In sales it is good to know what to say. Let's face it, a salesperson's number one tool is his ability to communicate. This is the same reason people are so concerned about public speaking.

Look, no one wants to stammer, hem and haw, freeze up, and not know what to say or do during their presentation. Communication and the ability to know the right thing to say at the right time is a definite point that counts to your overall professionalism and your success. These days, your customer can be just as informed as you are—sometimes even more so—and expects you to know what you are talking about. Also, your client is likely to have many choices that he may compare to your offer, as well as financial concerns that you will have to handle in your value proposition.

There will be times when you don't have the answer to your client's question. That's OK. How you answer is the key. If you don't know something, you could say, "I don't know," or you could say, "Great question. Let me get that information for you." Which one is more effective? You might think there is not much difference, but I assure you they are completely different. One communicates that you don't know the answer, and you lose credibility. The other acknowledges the communication and shows your willingness to serve! Being in a position to know how to respond to anything requires that you continue to brush up constantly on your communication skills and maintain a positive attitude and your product knowledge.

Selling does have a similar requirement to public speaking. If you don't know what to say, it won't go well! Know your presentation, work it out, and know it so well that you can handle any situation. Also be prepared for EVERY possible question, objection, stall, obstacle, delay, and customer question possible. Every time I hear something new from a client that I have not heard before or was not prepared for, I write it down, and then in my private time I prepare a number of responses that I can use in the future to help me handle that situation the next time I hear it.

Remember—you are in a business where communication is your number one weapon. You can't help anyone if you can't effectively communicate with them. This requires that you are prepared for anything and everything and have a sensible and logical response that furthers your cause and makes you, your product, and your company look good.

I'll never forget a kid who came door-to-door in my neighborhood to sell some kind of supposed amazing organic cleaner. I was busy with calls and projects at my home office one morning, and the front buzzer started ringing. Frustrated, I stopped what I was doing and answered the door. This kid is cold-calling the neighborhood, pitching household cleaners—tough gig! I have a special admiration for anyone who sells door-to-door, especially the young kids, but I was busy and didn't have any interest. I told him I had no interest. As I was shutting the door on him, he looked at me, smiled, and said, "I understand, Boss. Just give me sixty seconds to show you what it can do." As he's telling me this he drops to his knees and starts to apply the cleaner to a stain on the stone at the door. He looks at me and says, "I'm out here getting doors slammed in my face just hoping that if I work hard enough I can live like you one day!" The next thing you know, I was paying him $200 for a product I had no interest in five minutes earlier.

He had me at "Boss" and a smile when I tried to shut the door in his face, but he closed me because he was prepared, which allowed him to move into his presentation, demonstrate his product, and then close. Be prepared so that you ALWAYS have a response for every situation.

OVERWHELMED BY CUSTOMER OBJECTIONS

Objections can take place in lots of different places for a

salesperson: When you are trying to get the appointment with the decision maker, while presenting your product, in the negotiations, and in the close. You are always going to feel weak or fearful of being overwhelmed by objections so long as you fail to practice handling them. There's no substitute for being a ninja-assassin closing machine. Literally, you need to drill, drill, drill on your down time. This should be something you prepare for constantly. Make a list of every objection you hear so that you are cognizant of what you might hear, and then practice handling them all in a manner that will assist you in making the sale. *The Closer's Survival Guide* is a great resource for providing salespeople with ways to overcome objections. That one publication has more than 126 different closes and responses to objections that will prepare you to handle almost any situation. You really have no excuse. If you refuse to invest the time to prepare, I assure you that you will invest time in missing deals unnecessarily. It's really silly when a salesperson says, "I don't have time for training, reading books, or going to seminars . . . I'm busy selling!" In reality, is he or she busy selling successfully or just selling and missing?! Regardless of how good you are, you still want the best equipment. If your profession were cutting trees, wouldn't you want to take time to sharpen your saw? Of course you would.

If you want to close more deals, make more money, and create more sales success for yourself and your company, then there's no substitute for preparing like you would if you were a third-degree black-belt ninja assassin closing machine.

Keep a diary of every objection you hear and immediately work out how you would handle a similar objection in the future, or refer to *The Closer's Survival Guide* to find an appropriate response. Then drill that response in until you know it cold. Suppose you hear the objection, "I need to check with my wife." Write it down, look for a solution, and drill it until you own it!

For example, if a customer says, "I need to talk to my spouse," my response would be, "I understand, but if your marriage is anything like my marriage, she knows you are here and you guys already discussed this. Let's get this done. Sign here, please." Maybe you think that's too much, too strong, or too pushy. The only reason you are thinking that is because you haven't made this response your own yet, and you have never been successful with it. Had you used it a hundred times and had it work fifty, you would not have the "no way" response.

I am assuming that you believe in your product, your company, and yourself, and that you know all the value and benefits of it. Here's the deal—your prospect is there in front of you for a reason. He's looking to solve his problems with your product. When you don't know what to say to any objection, you are going to retreat, and then you fail to seize the situation and help your client. Anyone who needs to talk to his wife to make a decision, talks to his wife to consider one. (Sorry if I offended you!)

If you experience getting overwhelmed by the prospect's problems, situations, and objections, it is because you are not preparing yourself for the close well enough.

FEELING LIKE AN IDIOT

If you've ever had any version of the dream of being in front of a group of people and then realizing you are naked, then you know what it is like to feel like an idiot. You're caught, pants down.

People are laughing at you and you feel frozen. Here's the good news: Everyone fears that they will be exposed, caught, and shown to be inadequate or unprepared.

The word "idiot" comes from Latin. It was used to describe a common person who was not educated and not worldly. It is a word used to make a person feel bad, feel like he is missing out on something that "everyone else knows!" Feeling like an idiot is just the feeling of not knowing something. Oftentimes, we even intuitively DO know something, but we don't act on it for whatever reason. You KNEW you shouldn't have gone out to the bar that night, but you did anyway, and when you wound up in a bar fight, you felt like an idiot because you didn't listen to your own instincts. The degree to which you *fear* feeling like an idiot is the degree to which you look to others for your self-worth. If you do something that is idiotic, the best thing you can do is quickly admit it and learn from it so you can move forward the next time.

Look, what I'm saying here is that being an idiot and the fear of being an idiot are two separate things. Everyone is an idiot at some point and in some endeavor, meaning you have to become educated and worldly—you're not born that way. Great men of ability started out as idiots before they learned, practiced, and became great. But your *fear* of being an idiot will keep you from learning, practicing, and eventually becoming great. So go ahead, be an idiot and make mistakes. Free yourself from the fear of this by pursuing your ambitions and being willing to be an idiot. In this way, you will have the rare freedom of being able to stand naked in the face of judgment, and you will have a good time.

MEETING NEW PEOPLE

Overall, by survey, salespeople feel meeting new people to prospect is challenging. This is usually a symptom of thinking small and conservatively and following a *contraction* plan instead of an *expansion* plan. For example, do you know a salesperson who packs his lunch each day and eats at his desk to "save money?" Such an individual is withdrawing in life, not reaching.

The solution to meeting new people and prospects is to reach *way* out. Think expansive, not contractive. Where can I go today to meet prospects for my product? Where do you go in the course of your day to be seen and possibly get lucky? Get out and have lunch at a restaurant, not with a fellow salesperson. He's not buying anything from you. Get out in the world where there are people, and meet them. How about your gym, city council, church, conventions, industry trade shows, or classes you take, whether they are related to your profession or just something to do for fun? I have never sold a client watching TV in my home!

The possibilities are endless if you are actually involved in living life. The first step is to commit to getting out among people. The second step is figuring out how to establish communication with someone you meet. The easiest way for me to meet and develop a relationship with people is to visit the same place over and over until I am comfortable with the settings and it is natural to start communicating with others. Then, if you just take notice of something you have in common with others and comment on it, you will see the communication start up. Also, asking people for help is a great way to get the communication flowing. This could be as simple as mentioning the fact that you like the shoes of someone standing in the grocery line or asking them where they got their shoes. They may be wearing a brand of sunglasses you like or driving a car you want to know something about. If you are in a restaurant, you can even admire the dish the person at the table next to you ordered and ask about it. The point I am trying to get you to see here is that the more you are participating in life and taking an interest in other people around you, the more you will meet people. Be interested in others, communicate with everyone, reach out by being seen and making contact, and watch your pipelines start to fill up.

BREAKING THE ICE

It is always the salesperson's duty to break the ice when establishing a relationship. Customers have not called you or driven to your company or agreed to an appointment because they are not interested; if you are going to help customers get what they want, you need to get to know them. Sometimes just breaking the ice is a bit uncomfortable. The more you do it, the more comfortable you will become, and the more you believe in what you are doing, the less of an issue it will be.

Many times your prospective clients are guarded when they are shopping or when you are calling on them due to previous bad experiences with salespeople. You need to know how to approach prospects to make them feel welcome and at ease without turning them off or making them feel pounced on. It's simpler than you think: (1) Approach the prospect; do not wait for the customer to approach you; (2) smile, and thank the person for their time ("really appreciate you coming here or making time for me"); (3)

stick out your hand and say, "My name is _____," and ask for theirs if necessary. Keep your hand out there until the person shakes it; make physical contact where you can, as it breaks that physical boundary. Smile and keep smiling regardless of their attitude.

Once the communication line has been established, immediately move into explaining what your goal or purpose is with the time the person is giving you. Once you break the ice, do not spend the next thirty minutes building rapport and wasting your client's time. There is always time for that later! Before you present your product or company, take interest in the client by finding out what problem he is trying to solve with your service or product or by even making the time to see you. If Bob agrees to see me, then he is trying to solve some problem.

STAYING MOTIVATED

One of the questions I get a lot from people of *all* industries and careers is, "How can I stay motivated, especially when I don't feel like I am getting anywhere?" This is not a unique problem to salespeople; it's a universal challenge experienced by anyone trying to accomplish any goal. Whether you are trying to make that big sale, trying to lose those extra pounds, training for a marathon, or learning a language, disappointments and failures occur along the way to any worthwhile aim.

The key to success is knowing how to stay motivated in the face of barriers, stops, and things not going quite the way you'd hoped or planned. The number one way for me to stay motivated is to stay busy moving quickly from one activity to the next without a lot of time in between. You know the old adage, "Is your glass half empty or half full?" The reality is if you are moving fast enough, it won't matter because you are going to the next activity. My motivation comes from my attention on the future, not from something done in the past.

When I am moving on to the next thing, I don't have time to get sucked into focusing on what went wrong. Instead, I concentrate on what I have to do next. I believe a lot of depression is actually a mislabeling of inactivity! If there is a fire in your kitchen, I assure you that you won't be depressed. You will be consumed with putting that fire out or watching your house burn down. You might be depressed later, but not while it's happening!

The other thing with staying motivated is you need to stay away from bad news and doomsayers. Their goal is to drag you down and make sense of where they live and the choices they have made. They will only leave you feeling like more of a failure, more hopeless, and more apathetic about taking any more action toward your goal. Instead, stay positive, keep connected to people on your team, in your group, or via training who share your goal and who will help you celebrate your little victories on your way to the big win.

STARTING OVER WITH NEW CLIENTS

Making a brand new start can cause anxiety and uncertainty. If you are starting over with a new product or new company and need to get back to square one, it can make you feel defeated. When you find yourself in this situation, the thing to do is make a plan and, most important, get into action! If you are starting over, you have already been at the beginning point and gotten past it. You know what to do. Make your prospect list, work your power base, get up to speed on your new product or service, and get started! Get into action fast. The faster you start presenting your pitch, getting interest, and building your pipeline, the quicker you will work your way out of the condition of being unknown and brand new. Get your name, product, and message out right away. Don't wait to become an expert on your new product or company. Know enough that you yourself are sold on the product, and go make it known to others.

LOSING BUSINESS TO OTHERS

It can be demoralizing to lose a deal to a competitor. You have two choices of action when this happens: (1) You can blame something or someone else and be a victim, or (2) you can learn from it and win the next one. If you choose the first plan of action, it actually makes you worse. The reason for this is that you are not taking full responsibility for making the sale. You are allowing the consideration to creep into your thinking that something or someone other than yourself is in control of the transaction. This leaves too much room for failure and opens the door to your competitor to keep swooping in and winning your deals. Instead, when you have lost a deal to a competitor, try choosing path number two. Take a good look at what happened and why the competitor's product or service looked superior to yours. It may just be in the presentation. A great tool to use in getting this information is to have someone other than yourself, preferably a manager, make a "What happened?" call to the client. This is a nonthreatening call, which is not pushing for the sale, but is done more along the lines of a quality-control procedure to find out how the customer's experience was and how the sales team did in representing the company. This is very effective and can garner some valuable information that you can learn and put to use in the future. The difference is that this puts you at cause, as you are actually doing something about it instead of crying in your milk like a little bitch.

LACK OF CONSISTENCY

Your lack of consistency always boils down to a lack of real discipline. Discipline is not some concept for body builders and military personnel. Discipline is part and parcel of our everyday lives—it means you have exerted some control over random elements and made something of them. You would need to discipline an unruly garden to turn it into a thing of beauty in the same way you need to discipline yourself as a salesperson.

Your process of making the phone calls, reaching out to new people, handling a customer correctly from the beginning, following up—these are all things that merely become part of your existence when you learn your craft, train, and grow stronger. Your fears are like weeds in a garden, which grow out of control if you lack the discipline to contain them. There are a finite number of things that you must do every day, and when you do them, an incredible blooming occurs of your successes and income! If you don't do them, you will become overwhelmed by weeds, decay, and unruliness, and you will be scared to even try because you lack control.

Take control each day and DO what's needed. Create a checklist for yourself and make sure you reach and exceed each target, and then better yourself the next day. Calls to twenty-five people: DONE. Give my business card to thirty new people: DONE. Write fifty e-mails to clients: DONE. Demonstrate my product to ten people in person: DONE. Close three new deals: DONE.

Treat these items as a game and improve your "score" every day. Soon, the dreaded need for "discipline" will be replaced by fine-tuned habits that create wealth for you, your family, and your business.

COLD-CALLING/PROSPECTING

Who is my customer? This is a question all salespeople ponder when looking for prospects and a starting point for their business. You will innately have this answer the moment you fully understand and are sold on your product yourself. You see, once you are sold on your product, you will know all the problems that, product solves. Then you are armed with all the information you need to talk to ANYONE about the product or service you are selling. You will know immediately who has problems that can be resolved with your product or service, and you can target those people in your cold-calling and prospecting. How do you cold-call? Step one: Leave your fear, reservation, and inhibition at home. Step two: Look professional. Step three: Map out several potential clients based on who needs your product or service. Step four: Just go visit them! Be confident as you arrive. I have some real road warriors who work for me in my organization, and they cold-call in cities they are unfamiliar with every day. Their complete belief in the fact that our product can improve the lives of our customers gives them the confidence and courage they need to overcome any fear they may have and call on total strangers They walk into a company, bypass the salespeople, and go straight to the decision maker's office just by the manner in which they carry themselves. They exude an air of "I belong here, I know where I'm going." Believe in your product or service and negate your fear by getting into action. Pure, massive action will drown fear in no time.

COMMISSION ONLY/NO SECURITY

Growing up, we were all taught to study hard, get a good education, land a job with a major company, work nine to five, take two weeks vacation a year, and retire with money in the company subsidized 401k. This was the "safe" thing to do when planning for your future. Parents, teachers, and counselors preached this philosophy to countless students who were fighting to paint, dance, create video games, and think outside the box. As it turns out, this is a very dangerous course to take in life. Putting your future in the hands of the stock market and the CEOs of the large banks that rule the commerce of our society is actually a very precarious state. Witness the events in 2008 when even the giants like Lehman Brothers, JPMorgan Chase, and Merrill Lynch were stung by huge losses and had to close thousands of locations and lay off millions of people. What we have come to value as secure and safe jobs no longer actually exist. The truth is, it has always been the innovators, the idea people, the creators of new technologies who have fared the best in our global economy. So when you get cold feet and start to worry about the insecurity of living on commission only, consider this: Would you rather depend on the board of directors, CEOs, and the Social Security system for your future survival, or would you rather rely on YOU? Who do you think is more vested in the standard of living of you and your loved ones, the presidents of the JPMorgans of the world or you? Your financial success is best trusted to the one person who has the most direct control over it, and that person is you. That is true security.

LONG HOURS

Working long hours is in the eye of the beholder. Frankly, as I've said before, you have the same number of hours in the day as anyone else. Rich men and poor men alike all have the same amount of time in any given day. The question is whether you are working for your dreams or working for others' dreams. See, the reality is that even when you go home, you're still working for something. Maybe you like to work out, so you're working for the body you want. Maybe you have a family, so you're working for them, getting dinner together, cleaning up, putting your kids to bed, and so forth. Maybe you go home and smoke pot, watch TV, zone out until you pass out, and start over again the next day. If this is the case, you are working like a charm for your pot dealer, because you are a perfect victim of the system and no longer in charge of your life. If I described you in this last example, please call my office and get some information on how you can get out of that horrible rattrap. We can recommend a book that will wake you up and make you feel alive again, more than any drug in existence.

The good news is that you're working 24/7, whether you know it or not, so if you can maximize your time toward positive actions then you are working correctly. If you are just half awake and "clocking in" to any part of your day—or your life—then a half hour will seem like an eternity. If you are truly alive, the captain of your own ship, and working for YOU and YOUR dreams, then a fourteen-hour day will seem like nothing.

It's all in your head, man, everything. You decide what you do or don't do, but DECIDE. You can literally change time if you allow yourself to wake up and smell the "coffee of your dreams." A career in sales carries a stigma of having "long" hours, but I ask, "Compared to WHAT?" In sales, you are working for yourself, you are in control of how much you make, and there is literally no ceiling on your income, no limits except the limits YOU put on yourself. So if you think that working for yourself is working "too long," then you need to examine who you really work for and put in a letter of resignation, effective immediately.

TRAITS OF A GREAT SALESPERSON

1. Is willing to be told no. "Can't make the shot you never take," said Wayne Gretzky. To be a great salesperson, you have to be willing to be told no and then allow people to tell you no more than once. Most salespeople never ask for

the order repeatedly, failing to even ask for the no, trying to avoid the very thing they are certain to end up with.

2. Asks for the order regardless. Believe it or not, the number one reason salespeople fail is because they just never ask, "Can I get your signature here and here, please?" Most salespeople believe they ask for the order more than they do and in fact never even asked the first time, much less enough times. They are probably trying to avoid rejection, getting a no, or failure. Or maybe the discipline of asking hasn't been developed yet. Many people who are unable to ask are operating under the false belief that if they are just nice to people, the people will buy from them. Only a very small percentage of the people will buy from you without you asking, and most will only buy after you have asked five times. If you are unwilling to ask for the order, you will only get the leftovers of those who are professionally trained to ask for an order.

3. Listens selectively. If you are one of those people who believes everything someone says to you is true and that what people say is what they will do, you will be a disaster at selling. People will say many things to you that are close to meaningless: "I can't afford it, we are on a budget." "We aren't buying today, we are going to wait until . . ." "We never buy at the first place." "I have to talk to my wife." "I'll see you later today." The list goes on and on. If you are a gullible person and just believe everything your client tells you is "the gospel," sorry, you aren't cut out for selling.

4. Stays sold on his or her own story. If you happen to be one

of those personality types that is easily sold on another's story and unable to hold your conviction and belief about those things you are sold on, you will suck at selling your own products and be great at getting sold on others. You are stuck in some kind of reverse boomerang universe where you intend to sell your story, products, or services, and then end up buying everyone's stories rather than selling your own.

5. Asks questions. If you hate asking questions and feel doing so is "too" personal or prying into someone's business, you will not make it in the field of sales or as a negotiator. "What is your income?" "How long have you worked there?" "Who is the decision maker?" "Why can't you do this?" These are questions you will have to learn to ask. If questions cause you discomfort that you are not willing to handle, this will determine your fate in sales or, for that matter, in all life negotiations.

6. Gets answers to questions. I know some salespeople who don't mind asking questions, but they never take the time to actually get an answer. These people believe they are controlling the conversation by asking questions, but they fail as salespeople because they never insist on the answers. They ask a question and then ask another, sometimes answering questions themselves for the customer and never getting anywhere. The person who controls the sale is not the person simply asking questions, but the person who can get answers to questions.

7. Knows that price is not the issue. If you believe the lowest price is the reason people buy things, then you should not consider sales. You should become a clerk at Wal-Mart or a

waiter in a restaurant. Cheaper alternatives can replace 99.9 percent of all products on this planet. Whether it is a purse, phone, TV, automobile, insurance, mortgage, etc., someone, somewhere can and will sell it for less. Even more of a reality is that most of the things that are bought and sold are not necessary to have, so if a person wanted the lowest price, the thing to do would be to not buy it at all. Too high of a price is actually a myth and not the reason people buy anything, but if you believe the lowest price is the reason people buy things, you should not be in sales.

8. Is willing to pressure and persist. If you are one of those people who became convinced as a child by your parents, teacher, and environment that getting your way is a bad thing, then you should avoid all sales jobs and any job involving negotiating, debating, or entrepreneurship. A diamond is only coal until the right amount of pressure is applied for the right amount of time. People will not separate from their money or make decisions without someone building value and then insisting on someone taking action. If you despise pressure or persistence, don't do sales and do not go into business for yourself.

9. Believes in selling as a good thing. Most salespeople actually believe that what they are doing is wrong and unethical, and because they believe that what they are doing is a bad thing they will fail at it. Even one small dose of this type of thinking will kill your chances of ever making it in sales. Great salespeople are proud of their title and profession and know that nothing happens on this planet without salespeople.

10. Trains and prepares constantly. If you are one of those people

who thinks they are going to successfully sell just because of their natural abilities and are unwilling to train and prepare, you will not make it as a salesperson. You can be an average salesperson, but you will probably die broke. Even great salespeople will be plagued with competitive threats, industry changes, and challenging economies over the life span of their careers, and they will find themselves at risk. To be great at selling, you will have to make a commitment to sales training, sales seminars and books, and staying connected to sales tips and sales strategies.

By the way, numbers 1 and 8 will not only ensure that you fail as a salesperson, but also that your life on planet Earth will be quite difficult.

ABOUT THE AUTHOR

Grant Cardone is an international sales expert, sales trainer, motivational speaker and *New York Times* best-selling author. He is known for customizing sales programs for organizations of all sizes and has positively affected hundreds of thousands of people and organizations worldwide. Fortune 500 companies, entrepreneurs, non-profit organizations, and individuals use his techniques and systems to increase their effectiveness and value in the marketplace.

Cardone is the star of the reality TV show *TurnAround King* and is a regular contributor on Fox News, CNBC, MSNBC, and CNN. He has been speaking to audiences around the world for over twenty-five years on sales, success, finance, real estate, and motivation. His dynamic energy and his humorous and fast-paced delivery keep audiences entertained, intrigued, and involved.

Cardone is CEO of two training and consulting companies and owns a real estate investment and development firm worth more than $100 million in real estate holdings. He has written three previous books to inspire those who want to achieve success:

The Closers Survival Guide (2009), *If You're Not First, You're Last* (2010), and *The 10X Rule* (2011).

Continuing the tradition of bringing innovative sales tools, technologies, and solutions to life, he launched a state-of-the-art, interactive virtual training center at www.CardoneOnDemand.com and www.CardoneUniversity.com.

The author is also heavily involved in civic affairs and has received awards for his efforts from the U.S. Senate, U.S. Congress, Los Angeles County, U.S. Army, and others. At MIT, Cardone recently addressed The Young Entrepreneurs Organization, with representatives from over 15 nations present. McNeese University has honored Cardone as a Distinguished Alumni.

He currently resides in Los Angeles with his wife, actress Elena Lyons, and their daughters.